brian

solis

mind

Foreword by **Bill McDermott,**
Chairman and CEO, ServiceNow

Transform Leadership,
Drive Innovation, and Reshape the Future

shift

WILEY

Published by John Wiley & Sons, Inc., Hoboken, New Jersey.
Published simultaneously in Canada.

For general information on our other products and services or for technical support, please contact our Customer Care Department within the United States at (800) 762-2974, outside the United States at (317) 572-3993 or fax (317) 572-4002.

Wiley also publishes its books in a variety of electronic formats. Some content that appears in print may not be available in electronic formats. For more information about Wiley products, visit our web site at www.wiley.com.

Library of Congress Cataloging-in-Publication Data is Available:
ISBN 9781394198597 (Cloth)
ISBN 9781394198603 (ePDF)
ISBN 9781394198610 (ePuL)

Cover Design: C. Wallace
Author Photo: Courtesy of the Author
SKY10082740_082724

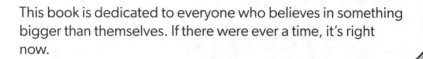

This book is dedicated to everyone who believes in something bigger than themselves. If there were ever a time, it's right now.

Ask yourself, how many life-changing events do we need to experience in our lives, before we decide to change ahead of the next event? How many disruptions that introduce uncertainty or even anguish in our lives do we react to or put up with until we decide to become the disruptor? How many people do we give unfettered power to in our lives, those who make decisions that we don't fully support or believe in, those whose actions do not reflect our best interests or aspirations?

You may not have the answers right now. You may not have the solutions figured out. You may not even know or understand the problems before you. But you do believe, deep down, that something better is out there.

Trust me, you will figure this out. That's exactly what these times of uncertainty and ambiguity calls for…a new type of leader. Committing to figuring things out is the first step to figuring it out, one step at a time. This is how you change the future and make things better for you and those around you.

You don't have to set out to change the world. Even the smallest contributions add up to something that matters. That's leadership. Even without having the answers, leaders figure it out. And the role of a true leader is to create a future that would not have otherwise happened. It's all a matter of perspective.

A better tomorrow starts with a mindshift. You unleash a butterfly effect when a mindshift becomes a gift you give to someone else.

This book is dedicated to you.

Table of Contents

Foreword

Hidden in Our Dreams Is Our Destiny
—Bill McDermott

I dedicated my book, *Winners* Dream, to my mother, Kathleen McDermott. I wrote that everything I was, am, or ever will be, I owe it all to her.

My mother was a fighter. She was a relentless optimist. She was the rock in our family and the inspiration in my life. She instilled the spirit of grit and humility deep in who I became as a human being, as a husband and father, and as a leader.

My father taught me about hard work, loyalty, and the dedication required when caring for others. As my basketball coach, he also taught me the importance of winning and teamwork. He believed that "none of us was as talented as all of us." And to him, winning mattered only if it was a *team* win.

People always ask me, "Bill, where did you learn your ethos to Dream Big?" My parents gave me that gift. And it was always up to me to do something with the values they engrained in me.

From my experience as a teenage entrepreneur to the global stage leading great companies, tenacity, audacity, and courage are the very things that helped me rise up at every turn, always with the relentless will of an underdog. Today, I have the honor of working with an incredible team of people at ServiceNow. Because all Winners need a Big Dream, ours is to be the defining enterprise software company of the 21st century.

We all have the Winners Dream burning inside us. If ever there was a moment to bring it to life, the time is now. Embracing that journey is not a question of "if," only a question of "how."

Here are a few humble suggestions from what I learned on my own journey.

For starters, there are many great role models out there. I have always tried to look for those who not only won but went beyond winning, leaving footprints for others to follow. Vince Lombardi was a champion in this mold. He said, "The only place success comes before work is in the dictionary."

We all need to embrace his perspective. If we want to succeed, there's no getting around hard work. In fact, we must learn to love the hard work. We need that inspiration to push forward, to define what success looks like every single day, and to chase it relentlessly. People count on leaders to know the way, go the way, and show the way. When they see real leadership, they'll pour themselves into following it. Always remember this: TEAM stands for together, everyone, achieves, more. We all do our part. We embrace the commitment to being lifelong learners, ever in pursuit of the best versions of who we are. That's when our unique magic goes to the next level in service to common goals and shared values.

When we are grounded in the love of work, we can expand our thinking about what's possible. Awareness of the world around us, and empathy for people, is the best foundation for human curiosity.

Let's acknowledge there has never been a time like we're witnessing right now. We survived a global pandemic. We are experiencing the rise of mainstream artificial intelligence and spatial computing. Disruptive technologies are accelerating and expanding faster and bigger with every wave. The world is changing in other ways that are unrecognizable, even unimaginable. No matter how much things evolve or change, we have something in our corner that will always help us thrive. . .the will to win, against any odds.

This is fundamentally a mindset conversation. Any way you frame it, there are certain essential elements that govern our capacity to shape the future.

One of those is vision. I have learned that vision is not only about what you can see. It's about how you feel and how you make other people feel. I have always treasured this in the context of leadership in times of change. People tend to overestimate what they can accomplish in the short-term, and they underestimate what they can accomplish in the long-term. A leader can open people's minds to the art of the possible. A leader can show people that the world isn't just changing; it's inviting us to reshape it. A leader can change the mood from uncertainty to positivity. And when the mood goes positive, anything is possible.

This leads me to the very practical reality of where we are today. This is no longer the time for business as usual. AI alone is a catalyst for the complete transformation of organizations, industries, and value chains that transcend traditional boundaries. This is a moment to rethink everything, from work to education to entertainment to healthcare—every job function, every role.

When confronted with such a moment, it's normal for people to shy away from Dreaming Big. I'm often asked, do I think we should concentrate on taking small steps and getting quick results? Let's be clear that we need to do a couple things at the same time.

We need a bold, comprehensive vision for what this world can achieve in our lifetimes. We need a compelling, exciting, and inspiring vision for why people's lives will be better in the generations to come because of the vision we set in place today. And yes, we need to have a solid grasp of the exact steps we can take to begin making this vision into the ultimate masterpiece.

Those who choose not to see a new way forward, who choose not to embrace the art of the possible, will find that business as usual leads down the road to irrelevance. For some, that may well come to be. For the majority, I see a brighter future. There are too many of us who believe in a better way. There are too many of us who have grown tired of accepting limitations or excuses.

That's the power of a mindshift.

This is about the fundamental change in the way we think and approach our challenges *and* opportunities. It's a transformation in our mindsets that leads to new insights and innovative solutions and outcomes. It shapes our ability to navigate uncertainty. A mindshift becomes the foundation for developing new strategies, for adopting new behaviors, and for fostering a culture of openness and continuous improvement.

I always remind people that what got us from there to here won't get us from here to where we need to go.

We need to open our minds and keep them open. We need to dig deeper, recognizing that the world's greatest challenges are our biggest opportunities. We should always follow the principles of design thinking and innovation: desirability, feasibility, and viability. This will help us harness the nexus of secular forces, all of which can be headwinds or tailwinds, depending almost entirely on how we choose to look at them.

I choose to embrace this moment. I choose to see it as the beginning of the next renaissance of human passion and creativity.

If we use this moment to catalyze our big dreams and begin to chase them with everything that's in our heart and soul, the world's best days are ahead. A mindshift isn't just a gift we give ourselves. It's a life-changing gift we give others to inspire and unite people. We help people become the best version of themselves. That's how we win as team. That's how we make the world work better for everyone.

So, dream big! It's a *Mindshift* moment! Let's do this together!

Introduction

Mindshift: Your Ctrl+Alt+Delete Opportunity

> # Your calling in life is not a goal to be achieved, but a gift to be received. This is your time.

We are living through volatile, uncertain, complex, and ambiguous (VUCA) times. While disruption has been constant throughout history, it's arguably accelerating today, driven by a confluence of new technologies, political and social upheaval, and a series of black swan events that keep piling up.

Thriving through this disruption, and all future disruptions, all comes down to your mindset: how quickly you're able to shift and get ahead of the next disruption event.

Your mindset shapes how you see the world—how you perceive the things that happen to and around you and the stories you tell yourself to help make sense of them. Your mindset determines how you process information and events, accept things to be true or false, and react to situations. How you visualize tomorrow is also part of your mindset, and your mindset very much defines the role you play in reinforcing the status quo or shaping the future.

According to psychologist Shawn Achor, "It's not necessarily the reality that shapes us, but the lens through which your brain views the world that shapes your reality."[1] How you react to challenges is really a matter of perspective. "We don't see the world as it is, we see the world as we are," Anaïs Nin wrote in her 1961 work *Seduction of a Minotaur*.[2] Our mindset can prevent us from seeing the world for what it could truly be, because it's human nature to see the world, the course of events, and the potential of disruptions as defined by our own life experiences. In times of great change, we tend to yearn for what we've become familiar with, and we lean on our survival instincts, often trying to beat back the transformations underway. But we can choose to embrace the change by changing our minds.

If we want to seize the day with disruption, to capitalize on a wealth of opportunities it offers, we need to change our mindset.

We need a *mindshift*.

What does mindshift mean? It's the opening of your mind and heart. It's your ability to see something new or differently; to learn and unlearn; to react creatively in times of change.

It's rewiring your inputs, expanding your horizons, rekindling your purpose, abandoning your comfort zone, and reimagining outcomes. It's exploring the art of the possible.

Over time, mindshifting becomes a discipline, a way of life. Mindshifting isn't a matter of just having a big aha realization. It takes intention and a set of practices for opening our minds and stretching our vision. The good news is, those practices are a lot of fun, and the results you'll see will be more than worth the effort. We are in a period of great opportunity.

Welcome to the Novel Economy: If There Ever Was a Time for a Mindshift...

During times of disruption, we often don't see how profoundly our world is being shaken up. What lies underneath appears like life as usual, but is actually an altered slate of human expectations, behaviors, and aspirations.

I began using the term the Novel Economy in 2020, as a way to jolt people's awareness about the degree of disruption and transformation we were seeing at the time. Through my work tracking disruptive technology trends, I had detected that we were reaching a tipping point of some kind, with so much roiling our lives: wars, disinformation and psyops, societal division, a global pandemic, climate change.

> "A new type of thinking is essential if mankind is to survive and move toward higher levels."
>
> —Albert Einstein

This new economy necessitates invention, innovation, and imagination. And it's a time when leaning on past assumptions, processes, and playbooks will only impede our ability to rise to the unique opportunities presented.

This Is Our Ctrl+Alt+Delete Moment

It's understandable that during times of disruption, many desire a return to normal. But we shouldn't be looking for normal or even a "new normal" or the future "next normal." Normal was the problem to begin with. Normal is striving for mediocrity, settling for the status quo. It's preserving the sacred cows.

Option A	Option B	Option C	Option D
Old Normal	New Normal	Next Normal	No Normal

If we instead embrace the new, we can achieve the extraordinary. We don't have to settle for the same old ways of living and working. Instead, we can seize this Ctrl+Alt+Del moment and reboot for a better future. This requires new leaders who can light our way through these uncharted paths.

If Not You, Then Who?

Have you ever hoped for, visualized, or even prayed for a desired outcome?

Have you helped loved ones, friends, or colleagues, not just because you felt sympathetic but because you genuinely believed that you could?

Have you ever read, seen, or heard something that made you think differently or choose another course of action?

If so, you have what it takes to be a leader in creating a better future, maybe much more so than you may think.

> "Leaders are fascinated by the future, restless for change, and deeply dissatisfied with the status quo. They are never satisfied with the present, because in their head they can see a better future, and the friction between what is and what could be burns them, propels them forward."
>
> —Steve Jobs

Now ask yourself: have you ever not pursued an idea because you felt like an imposter or that you weren't creative enough? If this is also true, congratulations; you're human. You're also still a leader and still very much the person who is needed for this moment.

Since 2020, disruption has left a deep mark on all of our lives—permanently linking our memories to visceral, emotional experiences. So many of us lost loved ones due to COVID-19. All of us have stories of struggle, learning, and triumph to tell. As we find our way forward, there is a unique opportunity to draw on these experiences to help shape a better future. The past is undoubtedly eroding. Many are looking around and saying, rightfully, "WTF!?" Some are fighting back; others are not paying attention or are doing their best to ignore the disruption. What about you?

You can either wait for someone to tell you what to do or believe in something and decide to go make it happen. It's up to you.

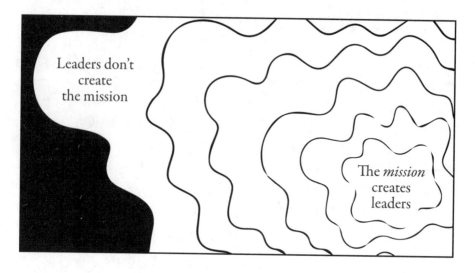

There are so many roles to play in reimagining the world. It may seem daunting, but the great thing is you don't need all the answers; curiosity is more than enough to get started. Every mindshift begins with a spark of curiosity. It could be as small as a "what if... ?" or a "why haven't we...?" or a "why couldn't we...?" As the saying goes, "If you want a better answer, ask a better question."

The spark ignites when you accept that you are not a victim of circumstances but are instead in control of what you do about them. You become convinced that you can help, that you can contribute, in some way, to an outcome you believe in. Of course, some things you can control, and others you can't. You can't control a once-in-a-lifetime pandemic. You can't control climate change. You can't control exponential technologies. You can, however, control how you attach meaning to these things and how you feel about and react to them. You can control what matters to you. You can control the intentional steps you take toward something different, better.

Your Destiny Isn't a Matter of Chance, but a Matter of Choice

I love the movie *Mr. Destiny*. Released in 1990, it stars Michael Caine and Jim Belushi. Its tagline asks the audience, "Would you give up everything you have for everything you've ever wanted?"

Belushi's character, Larry Burrows, lives what looks to be a normal, happy life. He married his childhood sweetheart and holds a seemingly good job as a sporting goods executive. At the same time, he's consumed by a painful memory: striking out in the last at-bat of his high school baseball championships. "What if I just hit that ball?" he constantly asks himself. He thinks his life might have been so much better.

On the eve of his 35th birthday, Larry's battered old station wagon breaks down in a dark alley, for which, of course, he blames not having hit that ball. He heads to a bar around the corner, where he chats with the bartender, Mike, played by Caine. Larry unloads about all of the problems in his life and how they're due to that infamous strikeout. Leaving the bar, Larry sees that his car has been towed, and he has to walk home. Shockingly, he sees that people other than his family are living in his house. Just then bartender Mike arrives—this time as a cab driver—and offers to take Larry to his new home. Mike is Mr. Destiny, and he's decided to turn back the tape on Larry's life.

The new house is a mansion. Larry also learns he's now president of his company, he owns a collection of classic automobiles, and he is married to Cindy Jo, the beauty queen of his high school. In this new version of his life, Larry not only connected with that baseball, but he hit it so hard that it shattered part of the scoreboard on its way out of the stadium, sending sparks flying over the field. He became a hero, and the rest magically fell into place.

I won't give away the ending, but as you've probably surmised, Lary comes to see that this new life is not really the life he wanted. This wasn't meant to be his destiny. Not hitting that baseball really had nothing to do with how his life unfolded. The key message of the movie is that we make our destinies; they don't just happen to us. They aren't preordained. We have the choice to build the life we want. Carl Jung, the Swiss psychiatrist, psychoanalyst, and founder of analytical psychology, famously observed, "I am not what has happened to me. I am what I choose to become."[3]

A mindshift begins with "what if I…?" instead of "if only I…."

From Wishful Thinking to Willful Thinking

Sometimes the hero you need is you.

Viktor Frankl was an Austrian neurologist, psychologist, and author of the incredibly popular book *Man's Search for Meaning*. Perhaps lesser known, he also wrote *The Will to Meaning*, which explored the question of why humans seek meaning in the first place.

"The fault is not in the stars, but in ourselves."
—Shakespeare,
Julius Ceasar

Frankl believed that the primary motivational force of an individual is to find meaning in life, or what he called the "will to meaning."[4] Here, we adapt Frankl's work not to unlock the meaning of life but to unlock change: the will to change one's thinking, learn and unlearn, and act differently. This is willful thinking.

If you don't like how things are, change them.

If you think things can be better, change them.

If you don't know what to do, don't wait for the universe to give you a sign. Figure it out.

Question everything, even (and especially) your own center of reference. Change of any kind always stems from questioning the way things are done or not done. Tell yourself, "Change begins with me."

In John Keating's stirring speech at the end of the movie *Dead Poets Society*, his farewell to the class of teenage boys he's taught to open their minds to new vistas, he says, "We must constantly look at things in a different way. Just when you think you know something, you must look at it in a different way. Even though it may seem silly or wrong, you must try. Dare to strike out and find new ground."[5]

Facing the Strange: Escaping Your Comfort Zone

Listed as one of *Rolling Stone's* 500 greatest songs of all time, David Bowie's "Changes" is more than just a catchy tune. Today, the name is synonymous with an eclectic and gifted artist who changed so often that it was his norm. He encouraged others to embrace change, to, in the words of the song, face the strange; to get outside of our comfort zones and become beacons of change.

In a 1997 interview, Bowie was asked if he had any advice for young artists.

> "If you feel safe in the area that you are working in, you're not working in the right area," he said. "Always go a little further into the water than you think you are capable of being in. Go a little bit out of your depth, and when you don't feel like your feet are quite touching the bottom, you are just about in the right place to do something exciting."[6]

It's only when you decide staying the same isn't an option that you discover the power you have to make change. But part of the challenge of rising up to lead is the ability to recognize that you are indeed worthy of the task. Feeling some fear about the road ahead in no way disqualifies you. It doesn't mean you don't have the self-confidence, or the bravery, to embrace the risk to venture into the unknown.

You can be afraid and brave at the same time. Just don't let fear overcome you. You can be a visionary and still doubt yourself. Just don't let doubt overcome you. You can be an optimist and still worry about the future. Just don't let anxiety eclipse hope and aspiration. You can be magnetic and still question if you deserve to be the one that others listen to and follow.[7]

> "I am afraid, yet fearless. For fearlessness is not the absence of fear, but the bravery to do it anyway."[9]
>
> —Runner Natalie Labir

If it were easy to take a stand, we wouldn't be stuck in so many places where change is desperately needed. Trust your deep-rooted belief within that, without you, the future will continue to be the same as it was yesterday. Without the bravery to embrace your inner champion, you are destined to wonder about what the future would have been had you stood up to say or do something. Pondering "if I only...."

In September 1947 the influential magazine *Reader's Digest* published the following freestanding quotation attributed to Henry Ford: "Whether you believe you can do a thing or not, you are right."[8]

If you're waiting for someone to tell you what to do next, then you might be on the wrong side of change. If you're waiting for someone else to do what you feel is best for the future, not making your own case for what you envision and why, you will find yourself on the wrong side of destiny. Don't talk yourself out of doing something great. And don't listen to those who tell you that maybe you shouldn't see your dreams through.

When you don't know what to do next, take solace in the fact that not knowing what to do is exactly the spot where learning, creativity, and knowledge begin. The act of courage isn't just about taking risks; it's unleashing curiosity toward the unknown. It's where you find answers to the questions you didn't know to ask or didn't know the world needed you to ask.

Ask yourself: are you eager to discover new ways of doing things? Do you want to plunge yourself into the future and let go of the past, at least the things that aren't working?

Yes? Then you are ready to be a mindshifter.

A Set of Mindshift Practices: Developing Your Vision and Leading Others

Becoming a leader of change isn't just about having the strength or audacity or pure courage to take control. It requires having a compelling vision of the possibilities and the threats. This vision should motivate others to work together, bring those possibilities to life, and proactively get ahead of the threats. Mobilizing them also requires persuasively communicating that vision so that others experience the same mindshift that's driving you.

Helping others share in visions for positive change has become my life's work. Over the course of many years now, I've developed a set of practices for mindshifting, which I will share with you in the chapters ahead.

You don't mindshift in the way that your car automatically moves from first gear to second to third and so on. You mindshift because you learn to pay attention, to be mindful, to observe. That's where you recognize the problems to solve, the jobs to be done, and the opportunities to capture. You don't just mindshift. You *learn* to mindshift.

I wish I'd learned how to do it earlier (oops...engaging in a little "if only" there...). Throughout elementary school, my teachers repeatedly told me to stop daydreaming, to "snap out of it." I don't know if it was something in my eyes or mannerisms or if it was just obvious to everyone but me that I would tune out. My parents were told repeatedly, "He's often not paying attention. He's too consumed by other things." Those other things were dreams, dreams of becoming someone important, someone meaningful, someone who would make Mom and Dad proud. But I had no idea how to pursue them.

I guess I always felt out of place in my youth and early adulthood. Though I always imagined a better future, in vivid detail, those dreams were all over the place. I didn't believe that the cards that I was dealt represented the hand I was supposed to play in life. I felt this in my bones. But I didn't know how to break free from conventional expectations, and I didn't put two and two together to add up to an action plan that would move me closer toward those daydreams. So, I put them to rest and did my very best to follow the recipe for life that was supposed to bring success. I achieved success that made my parents proud and provided security, but I didn't feel joy in my work.

It wasn't until I was almost 30 years old that I learned what it meant to break free from the status quo, to see through the mainstream standards of happiness and success, and to begin thinking more creatively—more disruptively. I had begun reading about how the human mind works, learning about foibles in our thinking, like cognitive biases. I learned how they blind us to the potential of emerging innovations and close our minds to new ways of thinking and doing. I dove into the literature about cultivating a beginner's mind and a growth mindset. I also learned the joy of rekindling our childhood sense of curiosity and wonder and how that helps open our minds to receive signals of exciting new possibilities. It was a fascinating journey of discovery, and in the chapters ahead, I will share the insights from it that allowed me to experience my first mindshift. They'll help you mindshift too.

This was when I found my calling, becoming what I've referred to as a *digital anthropologist*. I realized that I loved studying how disruptive technologies impact people's behaviors and how those changes in behaviors can result in massive market shifts. I began honing my ability to search for early signals, identifying emerging trends, of all sorts, and forecasting how they might change our lives.

Ever since, my work has been to continuously identify emergent trends that represent the potential to impact our lives, for better or worse. I then take those trends and break them down into a series of "what ifs" or "what abouts" to explore what each trend might lead to. That involves piecing together potential scenarios to explore how trends might impact a business, or the larger markets, and shift our trajectories. I then share these insights with executives, helping them to open their minds to the disruptions underway and the possibilities they present.

To keep my mind limber and open to nascent trends and to ensure I am making persuasive arguments to business leaders about them, I developed the set of practices I will share. They've allowed me to keep mindshifting as disruptions have just kept coming.

Making a mindshift shouldn't be a one-and-done thing. Once we learn how to open our minds to make a shift, we can apply the same tools to keep staying alert about changes on the horizon and seeing the new opportunities we can pounce on. There is never going to be a time when disruptions stop. There is also never going to be a time when mindshifters aren't needed to awaken the naysayers, the doubters, the deniers, and the outright resisters.

So, please join me, and many great thinkers and doers I've learned from, on a mindshifting journey.

One of those great thinkers and doers I've found inspiration from is Steve Jobs. In a stirring interview, he spoke about the power we all have to be the leaders the world needs:

> When you grow up, you get told that the world is the way it is, and your life is just to live your life inside the world...but that's a very limited life. Life can be much broader once you discover one simple fact...everything around you that you call life was made up by people who were no smarter than you.
>
> You can change it. You can influence it.
>
> The minute you realize you can poke life...you can change it. You can mold it.
>
> That's maybe the most important thing.
>
> Shake off this erroneous notion that life is there and you're just going to live it versus embrace it.
>
> Change it. Improve it. Make your mark upon it. However you learn it, you'll want to change life and make it better because it's kind of messed up in a lot of ways. Once you learn that [you can change the present], you'll never want to be the same way again.

So, let's go! Your courage is calling.

Chapter 1

Executives Don't Know What They Don't Know

> "The illiterate of the 21st century will not be those who cannot read and write, but those who cannot learn, unlearn, and relearn."
>
> —Alvin Toffler

Alvin Toffler introduced the term *future shock* in his influential bestselling book of that title, and he described it as a form of cultural anxiety, with both psychological and physiological effects.[1] Put simply, it's the inability to cope with the rapid and myriad social and technological changes of modern society.[2]

Future shock has run rampant within companies during in the wake of COVID-19 pandemic.

I had a very special opportunity to speak at the Hawaii Medical Services Association (HMSA) Employer Well-Being Forum in Honolulu about the future of work and employee well-being. Even though I was visiting paradise, the local companies were facing the same challenges being confronted all around the world. Particular issues were the Great Resignation, with so many of their employees preferring to leave their jobs rather than return to the office, and the phenomenon dubbed *quiet quitting*, with people staying in their jobs but said to be working less diligently.

As the world opened up, employers were surprised to learn that people weren't overjoyed to return to their traditional jobs. Nearly 57 million Americans quit between January 2021 and February 2022.[3] An average of 4.2 million workers quit in each month spanning from May to September 2022.[4] At the same time, nearly

89 million people were hired in a span of 14 months.[5] It seems that people weren't opting out of the workforce; they were upgrading or choosing a better path for themselves.

As for quiet quitting, in time, we learned it wasn't about becoming lazy; it was about taking a stand against employers who do not value the boundaries between work and personal life.[6] Professors Anthony C. Klotz and Mark C. Bolino, who studied the phenomenon, explained, "Quiet quitters continue to fulfill their primary responsibilities," but they are less willing to sacrifice quality personal time: "no more staying late, showing up early, or attending non-mandatory meetings."[7]

As a leader before Covid it was easy to see this as a reason for widespread termination. "Let's just fire them," many thought, even if they didn't say so out loud. After all, the job market was so competitive that they needed to hang on even to those they might have liked to boot. They would have learned a valuable lesson had they opened their minds to other possibilities about why employees were so discontented. The Great Resignation and quiet quitting were reflective of a large-scale reevaluation of life itself and how work fits into our lives.

●

Arianna Huffington,
founder and CEO of Thrive Global, emphasized,

"People aren't just quitting their jobs, they're rejecting the idea that burnout is the price they have to pay for success."

The Novel Economy is propelled by communities of employees, customers, and other stakeholders who are awakened, paying attention, and choosing themselves and their loved ones over the things that came before their own happiness in the BC era.

Unfortunately, far too many employers haven't awakened to the seismic shift underway. Some are willfully pushing back. But in many cases, they just can't envision a new, better employee experience.

When I work with executives at some of the world's most renowned legacy brands, I often observe that when it comes to emergent disruptive trends, they may not be intentionally pessimistic, cynical, ignorant, dismissive, or indecisive. Often, instead, they are so caught up in their own day-to-day pressures and deliverables that they don't have the bandwidth to dedicate their attention toward tracking and comprehending emerging trends, even ones already rocking their world.

This isn't an excuse. Executives *should* have a line of sight and resources dedicated to surfacing these threats and opportunities. They should be applying insights in short- and long-term strategic planning and decision-making. But their minds are stuck, replaying and replaying old scripts:

"We can't try that…"

"That will never work…"

"We don't have the money or resources…"

"We won't get approval…"

By stark contrast, leaders at Tuff Shed, a nationwide manufacturer of outdoor sheds, garages, and storage buildings, got creative. Like many companies at the time, Tuff Shed initially explored the scenario of letting staff go and shutting offices. The company was facing sales and installation challenges in March and April 2020. But by May, it was experiencing record-breaking sales due to a strategic pivot. They positioned sheds as instant spaces for remote home offices, remote learning, living space for relatives, and additional storage.[8] The company's leaders also recognized the opportunity to install structures to be used for testing at healthcare facilities. As a result, Tuff Shed enjoyed a hiring spree and reported record-breaking sales.

The Tuff Shed leaders went through a mindshift. They changed their mindset from that of being in a struggle to survive to one of capitalizing on the opportunity to thrive.

When someone tells you the change you're championing isn't feasible, it reflects their limits, not yours. They'll offer all sorts of reasonable sounding objections.

"We'll wait and see what happens…we have so many other pressing things to work on."

"We don't have the budget. "

"Market research doesn't show demand for it."

There are also, of course, those who just reflexively brush emergent trends off, "Nah, this all seems like a fad." Or they might make the common mistake of thinking that trends aren't applicable to them because they're emerging in a different market or with a different audience. Since a trend doesn't affect them directly yet, it must not be important.

"This is not for us," they might say. **"It will distract us from our core objectives."**

Excuse me. Without evaluation, how could anyone know it's not key to their core objectives?

Then there are those who "hem and haw." They're the catatonic executives who can't make a decision, whether due to fear or analysis paralysis. They're stuck and don't know what to do.

There's no way around this. Mindshifters will always have to contend with naysayers. I've seen them dig their heels in during every disruption I've tracked, for decades.

Here is a selection of the disruptions that have kept me busy over the years:

- **1994:** The consumerization of the Internet
- **1994:** The launch of Amazon.com and the dawn of e-commerce
- **1995:** The consumerization of digital photography
- **2000:** The dot bomb and initial crash of Web 1.0
- **2003:** The launch of iTunes and digitization of music, commerce, libraries, and ownership
- **2003:** The reimagination of retail design and experience with the debut of Apple physical stores
- **2004:** The debut of *World of Warcraft* and the consumerization of online immersive, virtual worlds
- **2006:** The rise of social media and Web 2.0
- **2006:** The launch of Roblox and the furtherance of immersive, virtual worlds targeting younger Internet consumers
- **2007:** The consumerization of smartphones and the debut of Apple's iPhone
- **2007:** The shift from subscription channels and rented content to streaming video with Netflix's online steaming
- **2008:** The rise of the mobile economy and the launch of Apple's App Store
- **2008:** Tesla Motors releases its first electric car and changes the future of internal combustion engine (ICE) automobiles while also reimagining the consumerization of buying and servicing vehicles (à la Apple, Apple Stores, and Genius Bars)

- **2008:** The shift from owned to streamed music with the proliferation of Spotify

- **2009:** The rise of cryptocurrencies and blockchains and the trading of Bitcoin starts

- **2008-2010:** The rise of the sharing and gig economies with the introduction of Airbnb and Uber, respectively

- **2017:** The further immersion into virtual worlds, currencies, and gaming with popularization of *Fortnite*

- **2018:** The introduction of "just walk out" technology with the launch of Amazon Go stores

- **2018:** The shift to short-form media with the globalization of TikTok

- **2020:** COVID-19

- **2022:** The shift to consumerized AI with DALL-E, ChatGPT, and the generative artificial intelligence (AI) movement

- **2022:** The popularization of the Metaverse, Web3, and nonfungible tokens (NFTs)

- **2023:** Google's response to ChatGPT with Bard

- **2024:** Google releases Gemini AI to up its game against ChatGPT

- **2024:** Apple releases Vision Pro to usher in the era of spatial computing

- **2024:** Humane, Rabbit, and Brilliant Labs release the first wearable generative AI devices

- **2024:** OpenAI releases AI video generation platform Sona and ElevenLabs releases an AI soundtrack/soundscape generator

Disruptive trends will only continue to evolve.

Every cycle has been the same. There were those decision-makers who were dismissive and those who didn't know what to do and stood still. I find it helps to tamp down my frustration to keep in mind that these attitudes are coping or defense mechanisms. Psychotherapist Peter Michaelson writes, "Cynicism is the bravado of the faint-hearted, the strut of the weak-kneed, the battle cry of a feeble voice."[9] Illuminating how fear is a driver of the defensiveness, American social and political activist Paul Rogat Loeb wrote about cynicism in his book *Soul of a Citizen* "Cynical resignation salves the pain of unrealized hope. If we convince ourselves that little can change, we don't have to risk acting on our dreams. If we never fight for what we believe in and aspire to, we'll never be disappointed."[10]

Working with many startups that disrupted their respective industries, such as Airbnb, Uber, Spotify, and TripIt, I can say that most of their incumbent competitors didn't see the threat coming (nah…, huh? no way! whatever!). Or they did see disruption ahead and just ignored it and complained about it later. Or they chose, maybe subconsciously, not to pay attention.

The problem isn't one only of old legacy brands. Even innovation giant Apple can be disrupted if not paying attention. Certainly, it wasn't ready for the market disruption caused by Spotify. The disruptors can be disrupted too, if they're not persistently mindshifting.

In late 2022, OpenAI's ChatGPT burst on the consumer technology scene, and with it, the mass proliferation of generative artificial intelligence (genAI) was born and rapidly began disrupting virtually every industry. Like Spotify with Apple, OpenAI's ChatGPT disrupted Google, which hadn't faced a serious disruption to its search business for decades. The impact of ChatGPT was so swift and menacing that it brought the company's founders Larry Page and Sergey Brin back into day-to-day operations, which they'd walked away from years earlier. A Forbes headline touted, "How ChatGPT Suddenly Became Google's Code Red."[11]

But Google search was already facing disruption on other fronts. According to one study, more than half of Gen Z women preferred TikTok, not Google, for search.[12] Prabhakar Raghavan, SVP of search at Google, said that "…almost 40% of young people, when they are looking for a place for lunch, don't go to Google Maps or Search, they go to TikTok or Instagram."[13]

This long history of resistance and denial can be dispiriting. Believe me, I know. But it also showcases the wealth of opportunity for mindshifters. Those who are closed-minded need you. You can become instrumental in motivating them to become curious about the possibilities of emergent trends. Even one voice, if creative, persuasive, and persistent enough, can spark a major mindshift. There's a long history of this, too.

Ford vs. Ferrari

Following World War II, the popularity of motorsports and speed-based contests exploded.[14] The United States was returning to normal, the economy was growing, the interstate highway system was under construction, and consumers were indulging their interests in horsepower. NASCAR was founded in the 1950s, and the mantra "Win on Sunday, sell on Monday" was born. Speed, performance, and winning directly translated into excitement, which resulted in more car sales.

By the summer of 1962, Pontiacs and Chevrolets were dominating all forms of racing.[15] Winning helped propel GM to capture 61% of the market share that year.[16] Meanwhile, Ford was reeling from a major sales slide due to failed products like the Edsel and the growing popularity of rival products from GM and Chrysler.[17] The company had become, like many others, focused on scale, efficiencies, and profitability, prioritizing shareholder return over innovation. A mindshift was needed to turn the company around.

Lee Iacocca, then Ford Motor Company vice president, was there to lead it. He was convinced that the company's current trajectory would doom it, and he proposed to CEO Henry Ford II that what the company needed was to be seen as a racing performance brand—as winners.[18]

Of course, Iacocca faced detractors full of doubt, skepticism, and scoffing. His idea was audacious: Ford should become a sports car company. And he knew how. The fastest way to do so was to purchase Italian sportscar and championship racing legend Ferrari. At the time, Ferrari was the most prestigious and fastest car around. The company produced the highest performance and arguably most sought after cars of the day. Ferrari Scuderia, the company's racing division and Enzo Ferrari's absolute pride and joy, had dominated one of the world's most daring and enduring races, the 24 Hours of Le Mans, held in Le Mans, France. By the time Ford approached Ferrari, the esteemed automobile house had already earned an unprecedented six (or seven, depending on timing) cars that attained victories at Le Mans dating back to 1949.[19] But the company was liquidity-crunched and in desperate need of a cash infusion, whether through strategic investment, partnership, or acquisition.[20]

> "Now I don't want to imply that we were building old ladies' cars. But something had to be done. I had only one thing in mind. We had to beat the hell out of everybody."[19]
>
> —Lee Iacocca

Nonetheless, Iacocca's ambitious idea to purchase Ferrari wasn't initially met with resounding enthusiasm. His mindshift and ingenuity weren't enough.

We've each been through this in one way or another. Even if we see the light, if we have our own "aha" or "uh-oh" moments, it's getting others to also recognize and share in the sense of need or urgency that becomes the true art of the possible.

Iacocca didn't give up. He needed to help Ford leadership, from Henry Ford II down, experience their own mindshifts to consider different options and solutions through a lens not biased by egos, stubbornly closed minds, or hardened hearts. He had his work cut out for him.

The 1953 Ferrari 340/375 MM at Le Mans

He confronted all manner of pushback. The company was already big into racing, in NASCAR. That didn't have the cache of Le Mans, though, Iacocca stressed. Who was Iacocca to be playing the role of the company's savior anyway? He was head of marketing during the worst sales slump in the company's history. Iacocca nonetheless persisted. Finally, in the spring of 1963, Ford officially set its sights on buying Ferrari. Lore has it that Enzo was not so cordial in his rejection to Ford, insulting executives as "worthless sons of [use your imagination here]" who managed a "big ugly factory that made big ugly cars" for a "pig-headed boss" who was not near the stature of the great Henry Ford.[21]

As you can imagine, Henry Ford II didn't take the spurning well. He was livid, his ego bruised. But he rallied. "All right, we'll beat his ass," he's reported to have said. "We're going to race him."[22]

Iacocca led the way with an alternative plan of developing their own more high-powered cars.

On June 20, 1964, Ford engineers wheeled the first Ford GT40 Mark I onto the show floor at the New York auto show, a revolutionary car that was built from scratch to beat Ferrari and exact revenge. "In going into GT racing, we feel we are accepting the toughest challenge presently available to the minds and talents of motor car builders," Iacocca told the press at the show.[23] While the Ford team failed to take home the victory at the 1964 and 1965 Le Mans, they learned how to adjust, invent, and improve.[24] In 1966, Ford defeated Ferrari, winning at Le Mans with a convincing 1-2-3 sweep, with its next-generation GT40 Mark II. Ford would go on to win four consecutive Le Mans victories, winning in 1967, 1968, and 1969.[25]

The 1968 Ford GT40. The car was named GT for Grand Touring, with the 40 representing its overall height of 40 inches.

The Ford GT 40 leading the race at Le Mans in 1969

Toffler argued that organizations that succumb to future shock do so by choice, not chance, and by the decisions leaders make and the decisions they don't make. Henry Ford II turned out to be a good decider.

Ford vs. Ford

Fast-forward to today, and Ford is once again undergoing a renaissance. That's despite the future shock of the past few years. It's also despite the resistance of many of its own dealers.

I first met Ford CEO Jim Farley in 2012, when he was appointed as the company's first executive leader single-handedly running marketing, sales, and service. At the time, Farley reported to then CEO Alan Mulally, who is credited with saving the automaker from bankruptcy in 2009. Eight years later, Farley became Ford's CEO. He's been described as a "blunt communicator" who's "not afraid to take some bold courses of action."[26] That was vital, because Ford was again badly lagging in innovation.

Tesla had shot into the future to make electric vehicles (EVs) sexy, and Ford was way behind. Farley quickly addressed the problem, announcing plans to produce new fleets of EVs and autonomous vehicles (AVs). Wall Street loved what it heard, and two years later, by the end of 2022, Ford's stock was up 70%.[27] Ford Dealerships, however, were of mixed mind. Farley understood that to compete against Tesla, and younger EV startups like Lucid and Revian, Ford also had to overhaul the dealership experience it offered customers. Tesla had dramatically disrupted the nature of dealerships.

Love Elon Musk or not, you have to admit he's a mindshifter of the highest rank. When Musk developed Tesla Motor's go-to-market strategy, widely available research and common knowledge were clear: if you want to make an impact as a new brand in a crowded market, connect with buyers and always deliver a better sales and ownership experience. Tesla set out to do just that. It started by taking over the site of an abandoned dealership in Menlo Park, California, and transforming it into an "industrial chic" space, with luxurious furniture.[28] I was lucky enough to attend Tesla's grand opening, and it was an exciting new dealership experience. But Tesla was just getting started.

Elon Musk at store opening in Menlo Park

Fun fact, this is my picture of Musk, taken on the day of the first store opening, which is still widely used in the press and online in stories about him.

Tesla further reimagined the concept of a dealership in its next two stores in California's Santana Row in San Jose and in downtown Burlingame in the San Franscisco Bay Area.

But Musk was intent to go even further. Tesla followed Apple's playbook and introduced beautiful immersive stores, which it located in luxury shopping destinations with high foot traffic, rather than the conventional "auto malls."

> "I love going to car dealerships!"
> —Said no customer, ever

In addition, rather than purchasing a car in-store and driving away with it, customers order their cars, whether in-store or online, taking delivery in the near future. The stores are designed as a destination for participating in Tesla's design aesthetic—to experience the look, feel, and style of Tesla ownership. What's more, buyers can configure their car with a wide range of customizations. In a brilliant branding move, by situating its stores alongside the likes of Gucci, Tumi, and, Coach, among other luxury brands, Tesla enhanced its own standing as an aspirational luxury offering.

Tesla stores and design studio

Tesla also introduced a bold pricing innovation. Musk believed in transparency about the cost of cars. One of the most irksome car dealership practices is jacking up the price of vehicles well over the recommended markup from their cost to buy them from the automakers. Ford had become notorious for this, and customers had complained vociferously. I felt the sting of this myself. When Ford announced that it was bringing the Bronco back into its lineup, I was thrilled. Though I'm an EV fan, I spend a lot of time in the Sierra mountains, where winter is brutal, with an average of 215 inches of snow annually. This new Bronco, the Raptor, would have all the torque and horsepower I'd need to brave the conditions. But my hopes were dashed when I discovered that all of the dealerships anywhere near me were selling the Broncos at way above the suggested price. At one dealership, the advertised price was $154,005 versus the recommended $79,005.

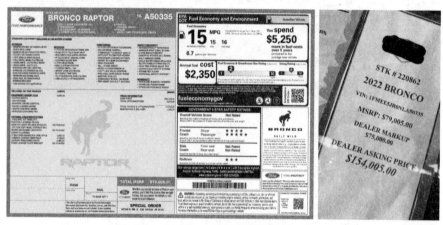

Ford Motor Co. 2022 Bronco Raptor window sticker (left)
2022 Ford Bronco dealer asking price (right)

With Tesla, the price you see online is the price you pay, depending on the specifications you've selected.[29]

While customers loved all of these changes, many competitor franchise dealerships didn't take kindly to it at all. Instead of opening their minds to learn why customers preferred this path toward purchase and instead of learning how to adapt in order to compete, many of them filed suits to prevent Tesla from selling cars directly to customers. The result was that as of the time of this writing, Alabama, Louisiana, Nebraska, New Mexico, Oklahoma, South Carolina, Texas, Wisconsin, and West Virginia ban Tesla from direct sales. Additionally, Alabama, New Mexico, and South Carolina prohibit Tesla from offering customers direct service centers.[30] Tesla nonetheless has flourished.

Jim Farley decided to lead Ford through a mindshift. In 2022, Ford made a surprise move by splitting its consumer business in half with Ford Blue taking over the combustion engine side of its business and Model e managing its EVs.[31] Both companies would prioritize pre- and post-purchase transformation, though. CEO Farley said,

> ...And we're going to just shift, [from] the eCommerce platform that we don't have today, [to an integrated platform] so all of our e-customers have a very predictable experience, whether they're in a dealership or in their bunny slippers, and they'll have a very simple, transparent, very easy purchase process...and we're going to invest in our marketing model with an emphasis on post-purchase [service and experiences].[32]

Farley understood he couldn't stop there, though. He knew he also had to address the company's dealership problem. Ford introduced three types of methods to choose from when purchasing a new vehicle, depending on what kind of car you wanted to buy (ICE, EV, or professional/commercial).[33] Dealers hoping to sell EVs have to become "Model e" certified. This requires them to provide a Tesla-like experience, with transparent pricing and allowing customers to build their car online and have it delivered to their door.[34] That all involves substantial expense for dealers. Yet, as I was writing this, 65% of Ford dealers had agreed to the terms.[35] The others are opting out of EVs—not mindshifting as of yet. In fact, dealer associations in at least 13 states pushed back against the requirements, accusing Ford of "unfairly burdening its retail network and violating franchise laws."[36] Sound familiar?

The story illustrates that even when an executive boldly leads a mindshift for a company, some pushback, or at least inertia, will inevitably ensue. Some people will resist the future. But that's no reason not to forge ahead. There will always be others who will open their minds and join in your cause, no matter how disruptive what you're advocating is, *if* —this is a really big *if* —your vision of the future is well founded and you've made a compelling case for it. You will always inspire a vanguard to believe.

Just listen to David Vorcheimer, general manager of a Ford dealership in Mendham, New Jersey. When asked about why he and others had signed up to be Model e dealerships, he said, "Because it's the future of Ford Motor Company, the future for all car manufacturers, and we want to be part of that future."

Friedrich Nietzsche, German philosopher and cultural critic, famous for his uncompromising criticisms of traditional European morality and philosophical ideas associated with modernity, believed in this cause. He wrote,

> "The fact that something seems impossible should not be reason not to pursue it.
>
> "That's exactly what makes it worth pursuing.
>
> "Where would the courage and greatness be if success were certain and there was no risk?
>
> "The only true failure is shrinking away from life's challenges."[37]

Chapter 2

You Are the Leader Who's Needed

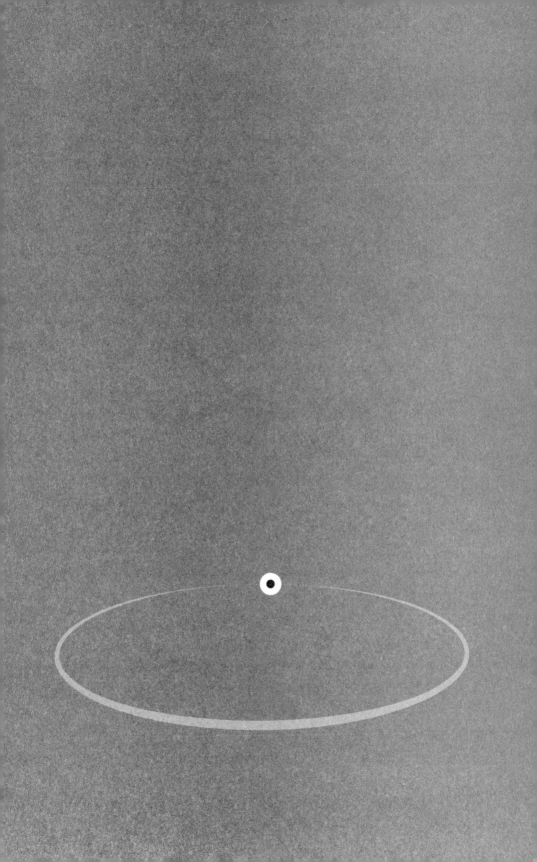

> "I am no longer accepting
> the things I cannot change.
> I am changing the things
> I cannot accept."
>
> —Angela Davis

In 2019, I published what I believe to be one of my most important reports, "The Digital Change Agent's Manifesto." It was the result of more than five years of research and thirty interviews with those who have led digital transformation initiatives for the world's most renowned brands, including Coca-Cola, Equifax, FCC, NFL, Samsung, Starbucks, and Visa. The report focused on those leading digital transformation within their organizations. I highlighted a number of change agents who were rising to the occasion and fostering change.

Before we continue, when I use the term *change agent*, I simply mean a believer in and catalyst of progress; this is someone who sees a better future and is on the cusp or in the process of becoming a leader. I am *not* referring to leaders of marketing or publicity initiatives masquerading as meaningful change.

The change agents I studied were often not officially sanctioned to lead change. They generally were not 100% confident that it was their place to speak up and champion what they were advocating. They were often reluctant to step up to leadership. Nor did they desire to campaign for a change-management role or believe in traditional change management. Many were not fans of corporate procedure, and certainly not of bureaucracy. They called to mind something Jony Ive once said: "I always thought that the idea of a company was a necessary evil to make an idea relevant."[1] He laughed, but he was serious.

These change agents ended up moving their organizations forward nonetheless, because they also shared the belief that they had an understanding of the potential impacts of disruptive technologies and they were willing to play a role in helping their teams and organizations capitalize on them. That fueled their transition from their comfort zones to conference rooms and eventually boardrooms.

They collectively described themselves as problem-solvers and critical thinkers. But they also differed in some traits. Some said they are extroverts and others introverts. Some said they find comfort in chaos and being self-starters. Others said they are cautious and need internal support and validation to further their efforts. In other words, there is no one type of person who can become a change agent.

My research found that change agents can rise from anywhere in the organization. No matter where they sit, they all care passionately about translating trends into actions. When I asked these leaders whether they were committed to staying at their current employers or might consider moving to the proverbial greener grass of a new company, they responded time and time again that they would stay as long as they believed they "could effect change here."

Change agents step up to lead mindshifts because they care so much about their companies succeeding. They pay close attention to trends reshaping their markets, whether that's evolving customer expectations or behaviors, changing employee expectations and desires, or emergent technologies. They seek to understand what's happening and why, and they explore ways to proactively respond.

At some point, a mindshift takes place in their career and they realize that they can't just sit idly waiting for someone else to rise and lead the way. It's their willingness and willful thinking that helps them evolve to become leaders, in phases, not overnight. They are not always skilled at first in getting buy-in, and most are turned off by the politics of organizations. They also probably wouldn't refer to themselves as change agents.

> "My passion is not as a change agent, because that role is more political,"
>
> said a senior director of innovation at a global luxury brand

Despite their aversion to corporate politicking, because these leaders realize that their expertise can be productive and beneficial to the rest of the organization, they put the work in to learn to navigate corporate relationships better and become skilled in the art of "managing up" and "managing across," with colleagues in different areas of the organization, to rally support and collaborate on the change process.

When I ask leaders who have successfully rallied their companies to capitalize on emergent trends how they've done it, they always share that they learned how to earn influence within their organization. They formed strategic alliances, focusing not just on managing their teams well, but on building relationships with key decision-makers, eventually including those at the executive level, even including those in the C-suite.

Over time as they influence positive change, they often rise into official leadership positions. Their ability to understand trends, their vision, and their ability to bring people together make them "heroes" in their organization, though they definitely wouldn't describe themselves that way.

Leadership Is Not a Rank, It's a Choice

This heading is a quote from Simon Sinek,[2] author of a bestselling book on leadership, *Leaders Eat Last*. In his research on leadership, he found that so many people in business who are in leadership positions are not truly leaders. "I know many people at the senior most levels of organizations who are absolutely not leaders, they are authorities." He points out, "We do what they say because they have authority over us, but we would not follow them. I know many people who are at the bottoms of organizations who have no authority, and they are absolutely leaders."

What makes for a true leader? I can find no better authority on this than Steve Jobs.

When asked about what he looked for in the people he wanted to bring into the company to help him lead the Apple revolution, he said,

> "The greatest people are self-managing—they don't need to be managed. Once they know what to do, they'll go figure out how to do it. What they need is a common vision. And that's what leadership is: having a vision; being able to articulate that so the people around you can understand it; and getting a consensus on a common vision."[3]

Jobs sought people who believed in better outcomes, not the traditional managed outcomes. In a later interview, he recounted:

> "We wanted people who were insanely great at what they did, but were not necessarily those seasoned professionals. We went through that stage at Apple, where we went out and we thought, 'We're going to be a big company, let's hire professional management.' It didn't work at all. Most of them were bozos. They knew how to manage, but they didn't know how to do anything!"

"You know who the best managers are?" Jobs asked. "They're the great individual contributors who never ever want to be a manager but decide they have to be a manager, because no one else is going to be able to do as good a job as them." He emphasized that they are doers in addition to visionaries. He didn't believe a person is necessarily one or the other. When he was asked in one interview about the balance between thinking and doing in innovating, he responded, "My observation is that the doers are the major thinkers. The people that really create the things that change this industry are both the thinker and doer in one person."[4]

You Become a Mindshifting Leader Because You Care

Another great voice on the nature of leadership, and one of the greatest leaders in history, was General and President Dwight Eisenhower. He was also an ardent fan of doers, and he was a consummate doer himself.

During World War II, in the space of less than two years, beginning in 1941, he rose from a middle-rank position as Chief of Staff in San Antonio, Texas to Head of War Planning at the Pentagon to Supreme Commander of the Allied Forces. Defense Secretary George Marshall promoted him so rapidly because he saw that Eisenhower combined great visionary thinking—being a master of strategy—with the ability to cut through red tape and whip even the most bloated bureaucratic organizations, which the Pentagon very much was at the time, into lean and limber fighting form. He was also able to get even the most egotistical of leaders, such as General George Patton and British Field Marshall Bernard Montgomery, to respect his authority and follow his lead.

> "My decision to attack at this time and place was based upon the best information available. The troops, the air, and the navy did all that bravery and devotion to duty could do. If any blame or fault attaches to the attempt, it is mine alone."
>
> —President Dwight Eisenhower

Eisenhower was in charge of the largest military operation ever launched, the D-Day invasion. On the evening before, he wrote a statement by hand on a notepad, which is widely recognized as a truly great act of leadership. The note was to be released to the press in the event that the launch failed. An indication of how much stress Eisenhower was under is that he mistakenly dated the note July 5 rather than June 5.

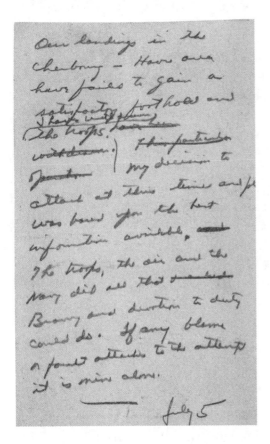

Eisenhower famously said about leadership, "What counts is not necessarily the size of the dog in the fight, it's the size of the fight in the dog." He believed you didn't need to be the strongest or most capable to win in battle. But you did have to care. You have to believe what you are doing is right, not just for you but for the people around you, and humankind more broadly. You have to believe that with passion.

Eisenhower with troops the evening before D-Day

Steve Jobs also stressed passion, and he saw it not as anything romantic, as only a strong feeling; he saw it as a form of pragmatism. At a 2007 conference, Jobs was joined by Bill Gates for a conversation on innovation and future trends. Each was asked to share his single, most valuable piece of advice. Jobs responded:

> "People say you have a lot of passion for what you're doing, and it's totally true. And the reason is because it's so hard, that if you don't, any rational person would give up. You have to do it over a sustained period of time. So, if you don't love it, if you're not having fun doing it... you're going to give up. And that's what happens to most people, actually. If you really look at the ones that ended up being successful in the eyes of society, and the ones who didn't, oftentimes it's the ones that are successful, love what they did so they could persevere when it got really tough. And the ones that didn't love it, quit. So, you gotta love it, you gotta have passion."[5]

Jobs then called this advice the high-order bit, borrowing a programming term that describes the bit position in a binary number with the greatest value. In other words, passion trumps all. As he said, "People with passion can change the world for the better."[6]

In his must-see Stanford commencement speech in 2005, Jobs commended the graduates, "You've got to find what you love. The only way to do great work is to love what you do. If you haven't found it yet, keep looking. Don't settle. As with all matters of the heart, you'll know when you find it."

Combat the Resistance Within You

> "Breaking out, walking freely through the forest, leaving old trails for new ones always entails a certain quantum of risk. Might we not come face to face with the lurking enemy? ...But both the forest and the enemy are within. Life entails risk. If it were otherwise, one could not bear to live it, for the risks of boredom, of being trapped within the self...of dying without having lived, are risks far greater than any that lurk in the forest."[7]
>
> —Gerry Spence

Steven Pressfield is an American author of historical fiction, non-fiction, and screenplays, including that for the movie *The Legend of Bagger Vance*. In his book *The War of Art: Winning the Inner Creative Battle*, he explores why many of us hold ourselves back from achievements we aspire to. The enemy is within, he writes. We all have the voice of a naysayer within us. He calls it the voice of resistance. When it comes to leading change, it's the resistance to sticking our neck out to be a champion. If we want to become a change agent, we must confront that voice and quiet it. We must come to understand that, as Pressfield writes, "Resistance's most diabolical trick is that it masquerades so convincingly as our own voice." A voice telling us that we're not the right one to take on the job. We become convinced by this voice in our head that this isn't our job, it's that this is the job for someone else, because it's too big for us to tackle.

We're not important or powerful enough to effect change. Pressfield goes on to explain, "We believe that these thoughts are ours, that they are an objective self-assessment offered up by our own rational, reasoning selves... They're not."[8] Rather, they are irrational thoughts induced by fear. But Pressfield advises that we can make our fear constructive; we can turn it into a powerful motivator. "Fear is an indicator," he writes. "Fear tells us what we have to do. The more fear we feel about a specific enterprise, the more certain we can be that that enterprise is important to us and to the growth of our soul." The irony, he points out, is that it's because we care so much about that enterprise that we feel intense resistance. "If it meant nothing to us, there'd be no Resistance."[9]

Part of the fear we feel is the fear of failure. I completely understand.

I hate it when I'm wrong.

I hate it when I make mistakes.

I feel bad about myself.

Of course I do, and you do too. This is how we're taught to feel after we do or try something that doesn't result in a positive outcome. We're taught to want not to be wrong. We stigmatize mistakes and punish people who make them. This begins in childhood.

Sir Ken Robinson gave a stirring TED talk about this problem. If you haven't watched it, please do; I can assure you that you'll love it. He's a master storyteller. Humble. Engaging. Funny. The talk is titled "Do Schools Kill Creativity?" and his answer is a resounding, yes they do. "We are educating people out of their creative capacities," Robinson says. His point is that by the time kids become adults, most have lost the capacity to be creative, to have original thoughts and ideas, because "they've become frightened of being wrong." This is also true in our work and how we run our companies and how we manage people.

But, as Robinson stresses, "If you're not prepared to be wrong, you'll never come up with anything original."[10]

Being an effective change agent doesn't require that you have all of the answers about what to do. It doesn't require that you are a genius visionary, who is supremely confident that you know the way forward. Even genius visionaries make mistakes about what they believe about the future, including Steve Jobs. As we'll explore more later, he was wrong, and emphatically so, about the future of the iPhone, arguing vigorously against developing it.

Being an effective change agent *does* require that you take the chance to speak up, to share your ideas, despite the fact that almost surely some of those you share them with will dismiss them, if not ridicule them. Take comfort in the fact that many great innovations have been scoffed at when first proposed. An article in *Business Insider* titled "7 World-Changing Inventions that Were Ridiculed When They Came Out" reports that in response to the news that Thomas Edison was working on developing a light bulb, a committee of Britain's Parliament issued a statement that the idea was "unworthy of the attention of practical or scientific men."[11] The other seven inventions mentioned? Coffee. Umbrellas. Vaccines. Taxis. Airplanes. And personal computers.

Who wouldn't want to be the one who endured some ridicule while pressing forward with these ideas?

Or consider the story of Amazon Prime. An engineer at the company, Charlie Ward, was annoyed with Amazon's Super Saving Shipping service, which offered customers free shipping if their order was $25 or more. As recounted by business journalist Jason Del Ray, what irritated Ward was that he couldn't use Amazon's convenient One-Click option for making Super Saver purchases.[12] "I'm a one-click addict," Ward explained. "I hate having to go through the order pipeline and choose everything again and again and again." Luckily for Amazon, Ward's frustration mounted and mounted. "I have a perfectionist type of mentality," he shared. "Things kind of irritate me and get more and more irritating over time." He thought Amazon should make ordering easier, and one day, in 2004, he threw out an idea to his team. "Wouldn't it be great if customers just gave us a chunk of change at the beginning of the year and we calculated zero for their shipping charges the rest of that year?" He recalls that the initial reaction of his colleagues was "Is Charlie crazy?"

What if the up-front fee charged didn't cover the shipping charges customers would otherwise have racked up? Even worse, what if customers ordered much more because they knew that over a certain amount, they'd be getting free shipping? They'd be abusing the program. The company could be ruined, some thought. But not Jeff Bezos. When the idea bubbled up to him, he jumped on it. How brilliant if such a program would motivate customers to order more! As long as Amazon could work out the right mix of fee and incentives to purchase, he perceived, then over time, the program could be a huge generator of sales growth. Bezos even considerably upped the ante on the idea, arguing that the program should offer two-day shipping, which few retailers were offering and would push Amazon's fulfillment capacity to the max.

Launched in 2005 with an annual membership fee of $79, Prime did cost Amazon dearly. But it also built great customer loyalty, and, over time, as the company added more and more features, like Prime Video and Music, just as Bezos had predicted, it became a juggernaut of growth.

Charlie Ward's crazy notion made its way up to Jeff Bezos because Bezos created a culture at Amazon of appreciating the input of people at all levels of the corporate hierarchy. He made it clear that he wanted them to speak up, even if that was offering criticisms. "Any high-performing organization has to have a mechanism and a culture that supports truth telling,"[13] he has said. At Amazon, one of those is a digital employee suggestion box, and Ward submitted his idea to it. Unfortunately, far too few companies have such formal channels for sharing innovative ideas. That is why it takes courage, and a strategy for building support.

But armed with the tools I will share, you can earn the influence in your organization to be that individual contributor who becomes a visionary doer.

Stephen R. Covey, a world-renowned expert on leadership and author of the perennial bestselling book, *The 7 Habits of Highly Effective People*, described leadership as the ability to communicate "to people their worth and potential so clearly that they are inspired to see it in themselves."[14] When it comes to leading a mindshift, we must begin with leading ourselves. We must cultivate our belief in our worth and our potential to be the leader who's needed.

Ask yourself again, "If not you, who?" And as you embark on this mindshifting journey, keep in mind the words of one of the great believers in the creativity within all of us, legendary music producer Rick Rubin: "Never say you can't do it. Say, 'I haven't done it yet.'"[15]

Chapter 3

A Self-Aware Mind Is a Shiftable Mind: Get to Know Your Mind

As I was writing this chapter, a friend of mine, Sarah White, tweeted, as if on cue, "My reading this morning was talking about how when times are uncertain or situations are out of our control, we start acting in a more defensive or victim way without meaning to. This was a great reminder we are our own biggest competition and challenge." When feeling anxious or when we're receiving pushback, we often allow our emotions to get the better of us. Keeping them in check is vital to effectively leading as a mindshifter.

To become more in charge of our responses, we must develop self-awareness.

Self-awareness is your ability to perceive and understand the things that make you who you are, including your personality, actions, values, beliefs, emotions, and thoughts.[1] Essentially, it is a psychological state in which the self becomes the focus of attention.

To be self-aware is to be conscious of how thoughts and feelings influence thinking and behaviors, both actions and inactions. How are we showing up in each moment? How are we responding to situations, opportunities, and threats? How are we engaging with those around us?

Research has found that through self-awareness, when we see ourselves clearly, we are more confident and more creative. We make sounder decisions, build stronger relationships, and communicate more effectively. And we're more effective leaders with more-satisfied employees and more profitable companies.[2]

Self-awareness is, like all else we're learning, a defining quality in the type of new leader we need.

The problem is that self-awareness is a rare skill. In fact, one study revealed that only 10–15% of people studied are self-aware.[3] Separate research demonstrated that most leaders are woefully unaware of their shortfalls. In a study of more than 3,600 leaders, the researchers found that higher-level leaders significantly overvalued their skills compared with how others perceived them. This pattern was sweeping across 19 out of the 20 competencies the researchers measured, including emotional self-awareness, accurate self-assessment, empathy, trustworthiness, and leadership performance.[4]

The power of self-awareness helps us gain the critical abilities to...

...see trends, threats, and opportunities more clearly and openly.

...respond and influence outcomes, thoughtfully.

...gain self-confidence.

...become better decision-makers.

...communicate with greater clarity and intention.

...understand things from different perspectives, empathetically.

...free us from our assumptions and biases.

...build more meaningful connections and relationships, which seed communities of like-minded people.[5]

The good news is that we can develop our self-awareness. That takes understanding more about it. Organizational psychologist Tasha Eurich has studied self-awareness, and she's found that there are two types of self-awareness: internal and external.[6]

Internal self-awareness represents our perspective on how we see our own values, passions, aspirations, fit with our environment, reactions (including thoughts, feelings, behaviors, strengths, and weaknesses), and impact on others.

External self-awareness reflects our perception of how people view us according to the criteria referenced. Eurich's research shows that people who understand how others see them are more skilled at showing empathy and taking others' perspectives.

Empathetic leaders understand better how to learn, grow, and relate with their colleagues as they embark on mindshifting. "For leaders who see themselves as their employees do, their employees tend to have a better relationship with them, feel more satisfied with them, and see them as more effective in general," Eurich found in her research.[7]

So, how well do you think you know yourself?

Eurich's research identified four leadership archetypes, each with a different set of opportunities to grow and excel.

Most leaders have few people around them who can provide candid feedback, and most leaders do not ask for authentic feedback. Additionally, the greater the power, the more fearful people are of offering constructive feedback. They're scared it could negatively affect their careers. Business professor James O'Toole observed that as leaders gain power, their willingness to listen shrinks because they believe they know more than everyone else.[8] On the contrary, great leaders listen and encourage candor.

For example, one analysis revealed that the most successful leaders employ 360-degree leadership reviews of effectiveness. This feedback can be really tough, and sometimes biased and unhelpful. So, a good practice is to seek feedback from "loving critics," who you're confident genuinely have your best interests in mind and are willing to share the truth because they believe that you trust them. It's also best to "gut check" difficult or perhaps surprising feedback with others to ensure that it's not coming from a rarefied point of view and also so that it doesn't spark overreaction or over correction.[9]

Pleasers **High External and Low Internal Self-Awareness** They can be so focused on appearing in a certain way to others that they could be overlooking what matters to them. Over time, they tend to make choices that aren't in service of their own success and fulfillment.	Aware **High External and High Internal Self-Awareness** They know who they are, what they want to accomplish, and seek out and value others' opinions. This is where leaders begin to fully realize the true benefits of self-awareness.
Seekers **Low External and Internal Self-Awareness** They don't yet know who they are, what they stand for, or how their teams see them. As a result, they might feel stuck or frustrated with their performance and relationships.	Introspectors **Low External and High Internal Self-Awareness** They're clear on who they are but don't challenge their own views or search for blind spots by getting feedback from others. This can harm their relationships and limit their success.

Combat Negativity and Cultivate Optimism

Have you ever asked yourself, "What is the dumbest thing I have to do every day?" or "Why doesn't someone take a walk in my shoes for a change?" or "Why couldn't someone see what was right in front of them the whole time?"

Be mindful of your perspective every time you ask these questions or others like them. It's questions like these that symbolize potential aha or eureka moments, which can spur intent and contemplation or moments of "hmmm."

But, if they are coming instead from a place of negativity, such questions can trigger fear-based behavior that fosters denial or anger or smugness. Ignoring or belittling these opportunities for constructive reflection and growth will ultimately, at some point, give way to the "uh-oh" realization that you've missed the opportunity to mindshift.

Ask yourself:

What's your default reaction to problems or challenges you face?

Do you need to develop more optimism?

Do you have a generally more positive outlook or more pessimistic?

The answers are key elements of your perspective about life in general, and how much you tend toward the positive or negative has a great deal to do with your success, as well as with effectively leading others. Getting a fix on this is a big component of developing self-awareness.

Our perspective defines how we translate observations and events into how we feel about them and what we do next, how we do it, and why. We can respond passively (huh?), ignore (nah…), dismiss (whatever), be cynical (no way!), stall (hem and haw), or be curious (hmmm).

Your perspective is shaped by learned attitudes over time that affect how you subconsciously think and act.[10] This creates implicit or unconscious biases that affect your judgment or behaviors without you realizing it.[11] We all have them. And a bias toward negativity is one of them.

This isn't something to beat ourselves up about. Evolution has made us this way. Rick Hanson, author of *Hardwiring Happiness*, shares how the human brain is wired to fixate on the negative instead of the positive; our brains were wired to consume negativity.[12] In his research, he found that we learn more quickly from our bad experiences than from our more positive experiences. But he also learned that we can change this. We can give our brains the space to focus on the good things surrounding us and rewire them to process information through an aperture of positivity.

Working on this will be invaluable for mindshifting. When it comes to your ability to recognize and effectively respond to emerging trends, negativity is a curse. When it comes to your ability to recognize and effectively respond to emerging trends, how you acknowledge and conquer your biases becomes an invaluable skill to master.

Start with reflecting on how generally optimistic or negative you are.

Do you take time regularly to allow yourself to ponder, "hmmm"?

Do you capture your ideas and consider possibilities?

Do you recognize opportunities for self-reflection and growth?

Do you see yourself as a leader or a catalyst or an enabler? Or do you see yourself more as a victim?

Do you find yourself repeatedly responding with "nah" or "no way" to ideas for changes being proposed?

Do you regularly talk yourself out of taking chances in order to explore new horizons?

Take a breath and let's keep going?

Do you blame others?

Do you automatically expect the worst?

Do you minimize things to try to make them go away?

Do you more often see the negative in situations?

If you've answered yes to many, or even just a couple, of these questions, it's time to work on developing more optimism. A negative perspective is toxic; it dampens your mood, restricts your outlook, and even impairs your decision-making. You will talk yourself out of something potentially great or talk yourself into something limiting.

Research shows negative thoughts have a big impact on brain function.[13] They impede your ability to think logically, which slows down activity in the cerebellum. If negative thinking becomes a habit, you strengthen the synapses and neurons that fuel negative thoughts. Eventually, negative thoughts and beliefs become so ingrained that they become part of your brain's structure. You have to work through this structure in any attempt to work through problems and challenges. This results in a reduced ability to think differently, to ideate creatively, and to come up with creative solutions. The more you entertain negative thinking, the less you can see your true potential and the potential in emerging trends.

Negativity also wastes a lot of energy. It is literally exhausting. According to a study by Russell Johnson of Michigan State University, negative-minded workers are more likely to become mentally fatigued and defensive and experience a decline in production. It can also alienate you from colleagues who could help you lead change. Cynics and pessimists are unattractive to those who are more optimistic, positive, and productive.[14]

Negative will always attract negative. Negativity is contagious and can infect everything and everyone in an organization.[15]

By contrast, positive will always attract positive.

Optimism helps keep your mind receptive. It also combats anxiety about change.[16] In addition, research shows that positive thinking activates more prefrontal cortex activity in the brain, which plays a critical role in our capacity to effectively manage our emotions, helping to increase our well-being.[17]

You can cultivate a more positive perspective by consciously listening to your self-talk and transforming negative thoughts into optimistic ones.

"This can't be done."	versus	"We can do whatever we put our minds to."
"It's impossible."	versus	"I don't have the answer, but let's figure this out."
"I'm not good enough."	versus	"We are worthy of better outcomes."
"I don't think I'll ever..."	versus	"I can do this" or " I am confident I will..."
"This will never..."	versus	"What if...?"
"I am not strong enough."	versus	"I am strong enough to start, and I can gain strength along the way."
"Who cares?"	versus	"We need to care because..." or "People will care because this affects them."
"There's so much that can go wrong."	versus	"We have to try because..." or "Even if we fail, we'll learn..."
"I am too busy to think about this right now."	versus	"I can make time to understand its potential."
"It's not that important."	versus	"This is important because..."
I'm not responsible."	versus	"I'm a stakeholder and will do my part."

Making these corrections takes practice. You have to stay alert about listening to your negative thoughts, because negativity can become a bias, with our brains reaching for it without us even being consciously aware. This is just one of a number of biases that can impede our ability to perceive emerging opportunities (more on that in just a bit).

First, here is a set of practices for mindshifting from negative to productive thinking. This may seem like a lot of work, but I assure you, doing it will be incredibly worthwhile.

Shift from the Victim Role to Being the Victor

To become a victor, find a victor's mantra. I remember stumbling across some lovely words of advice from 7 Mindsets. It serves as an excellent model to personalize for your victor's mantra: "I am not a victim of my past, my future is not predetermined, my life is what I choose it to be from this moment moving forward."[18]

Surround Yourself with Positive People and Inputs

You are a byproduct of who you spend your time with, what you read and watch, and who you follow and listen to. Pay attention to their cycles of negativity versus positivity. Find people who challenge you, build you up, and offer productive feedback to help you grow.

Identify Your Emotional Triggers

The key is to catch yourself before you say or do something negative. Practice identifying your emotions as they are happening (I know it's hard, but it's not impossible). Don't repress or deny them; learn to tame them in the moment. Learn how to become flexible enough to understand what you're feeling and why.

- Present solutions instead of problems.[19]
- State what you want, not what you don't.
- Reduce the use of exaggerated or overly emotional language.
- Try "I statements" using this model as an example, "I feel (emotion word) when (explanation)." I feel like I don't understand this, but let's figure it out together versus I don't get it. I don't know what to do.
- Be careful with the word *but*; it can often negate the previous statement or intention. Try building with *and* instead.

Consider How Your Actions Affect Others

I can't tell you how many times I've held off on sending an email or text until I had a chance to process what I was feeling. I'm always glad I do because when I reread what I was about to send, I'm often surprised at how much I let my emotions get the best of me.

It's easy to react in any given moment because we're human and feelings are complex. Thinking first, processing before we act, and being considerate can dramatically change any situation and outcome for the better. Consider how your response can be taken, read into, or misunderstood.

Practice Self-Discipline

None of this is easy. The best leaders are always learning, always seeking to improve, and exercising the self-discipline necessary to be resilient and positive and productive.

Now, about those other biases....

Conquer Cognitive Biases

You've probably heard about some of the cognitive biases that have been implanted in our brains through the course of evolution. Keeping ourselves mindful of these biases, so that we can stop our minds from falling into these traps, is another essential component of developing our self-awareness. Getting to know ourselves also involves getting to know the things about ourselves that we have in common with everyone else.

When it comes to cognitive biases, a particularly pernicious set regarding mindshifting is as follows:[20]

● Affinity bias

Describes our predisposition to favor people who remind us of ourselves. This unconscious bias causes us to gravitate toward others who appear to be like us.[21]

Conformity bias

A worthy foe to innovation efforts everywhere; can lead to groupthink, where people align opinions and behaviors to match the bigger group. Conformity bias tends to lead us into the infamous box we're told to think outside of, limiting creativity, openness, and growth.

Status quo bias

Describes our preference for the way things are and our strong desire to keep things as is and constant. This evolves into making decisions that continue the status quo and/or an unwillingness to change and can even lead to detracting or inspiring resistance among others to protect the status quo.

Overconfidence bias

Is exhibited in the "expert's mind." It's the tendency for someone to think that they are better at certain abilities and skills than they are. This usually manifests in an inflated ego, which impedes logical thinking and decision-making, creativity, humility, and collaboration. For example, in the face of disruption or emergent zeitgeists, the expert may overestimate skills and previous successes to address an entirely new set of problems and opportunities.

Authority bias

Is a net effect of overconfidence bias. Following a seemingly trusted authority figure without critical thinking may spread the negative effects of an expert's mind onto others. This means you can be influenced by an authority figure simply because of their stature. Consider when a social media influencer known for their popular fashion looks offers a medical opinion that runs contrary to your physician's advice.

Recency bias

Favors recent events over historic ones, placing too much emphasis on experiences that are freshest in memory. This bias strikes when people believe events or experiences in the recent past provide insight into how things must be in the future, largely ignoring disruptive events playing out before them.

Anchor bias

Is when someone holds onto an initial or single piece of information as their "anchor" to make decisions, rejecting (consciously or unconsciously) any information to the contrary.

Confirmation bias

Leads you to seek input and information that confirms or validates your point of view and is a tendency to pay more attention to information that confirms your existing beliefs. As a result, your perspective is limited to a purview that keeps you from seeing threats and opportunities that others might readily see and pursue ahead of you.

Phew! That's quite an array of mental glitches working against us. The truth is, we're probably all going to let these get the better of our thinking sometimes. But by staying mindful of them, we can get better and better at recognizing when our minds are being fooled by them. One powerful way of developing more ability to do this is cultivating a beginner's mind. For that, please read on!

Chapter 4

The Beginner's Mind

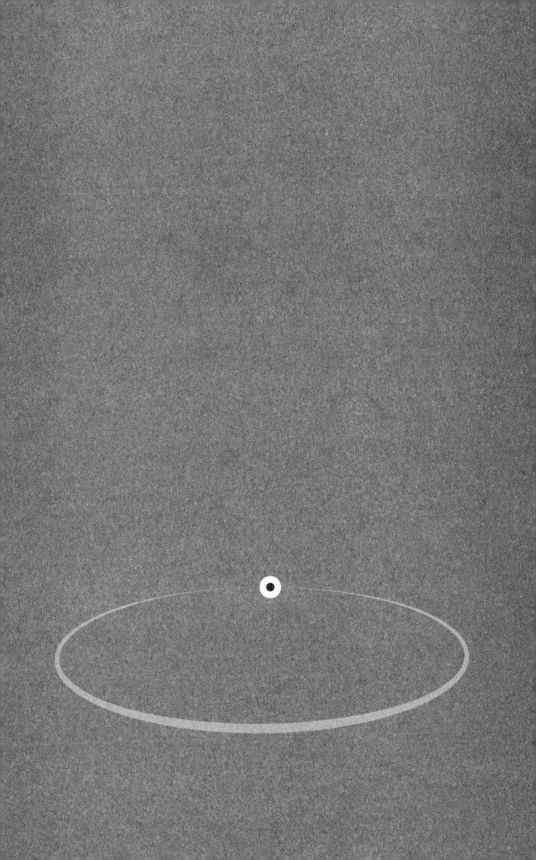

> # "There is nothing either good or bad, but thinking makes it so."
>
> —*Hamlet*, William Shakespeare, Act II, Scene 2

French novelist Marcel Proust, author of *In Search of Lost Time*, captured the gift of a beginner's mind beautifully when he wrote, "The real voyage of discovery consists not in seeking new landscapes, but in having new eyes."[1] It requires work to free our minds not only from the mental biases we're all inflicted by but from our own experience.

A Lesson in Mindshifting More Than 100 Years in the Making

On the fateful night of April 14, 1912, Captain Edward Smith was determined to surprise the horde of media he knew would be waiting at the port in New York where the glorious *Titanic* would berth. He didn't want to just arrive on time; he wanted to show up early. Though he knew the northern Atlantic was strewn with icebergs, he was confident he and his crew would spot any that might present danger with enough time to steer around them. Even though more than 30 different warnings were sent to the ship about how densely packed with bergs the sea had become, Smith maintained a high speed. He did change course, heading slightly south, but that was too little, much too late.[2]

The *Titanic* plowed into the side of an enormous iceberg at 11:40 p.m. The ice raining down on the deck as the ghostly mountain loomed before them must have been a surreal sight. Was it just a grazing? Had the unsinkable hull held strong?

The *Titanic* leaving Southampton, England, April 10, 1912

Captain Edward John Smith on the *Titanic* bridge on the morning of April 10, 1912

Hopes were high as the ship moved on. But all too soon, the ship's designer, Thomas Andrews, having surveyed the damage, reported that five compartments of the hull were flooding, whereas the ship had been built to remain afloat with up to four compartments filled. He estimated the ship would sink in about one to two hours, though the final descent of the bow, spiked dramatically heavenward, took longer.[3] Many survivors reported that the sinking played out like a tragic play, over the course of almost three hours from the point of impact—the duration of most stage plays in that era.

Smith was captaining a brand new ship with a novel design. But he didn't bring a new mindset to the mission. He apparently didn't open his mind to the possibility that this massive ocean liner, the largest built at that time, might not maneuver as readily as he was used to. As the treasure hunter Bock Lovett says in the James Cameron blockbuster film about the sinking, Smith had "26 years of experience working against him."[4]

There's a famous quote by Abraham Maslow, "If the only tool you have is a hammer, you tend to see every problem as a nail." "Everything we know" attacks different problems and opportunities with the same mindset and approach.

I don't know that I've ever encountered anyone who self-identifies as "close-minded." But the fact is, our minds have been built to resist new information, especially when it refutes our prior experience or goes against our beliefs. In 2016, neuroscientists at USC's Brain and Creativity Institute, Jonas T. Kaplan, Sarah I. Gimbel, and Sam Harris, studied how the brain reacts when one's political beliefs are challenged. The scientists used MRI technology to scan the brains of 40 participants, watching their brain chemistry as their team tried to sway the participants' political positions. The parts of the brain that were triggered control deep, emotional thoughts about personal identity.[5]

Kaplan said of the findings, "Their brains were emotionally threatened and went into defense mode, shutting down any willingness to accept counter arguments," explaining that generally, "when people [are] being challenged, they're less likely to change their minds."[6] Another of the researchers, Max Henning, commented, "People don't often realize how automatic it can be to push back on information that you disagree with, even if you identify as a person that is open to new ideas."[7] That's in part because we tend to surround ourselves with people like us, which fortifies our beliefs. When we're surrounded by similar beliefs, we're rarely challenged.

Opening our minds up is also hard because it is a form of shifting our identity. When we engage in questioning what we've learned from our experiences and interrogating our beliefs, we can feel unmoored. Either we can decide to accept that discomfort and sail forward or we can stay tethered to old ways and become obsolete. Just think of all the leaders in business that failed to embrace change: Blackberry, Nokia, Blockbuster, Toys R Us, Borders, General Motors (yes, even though it's still here today, a new company took over in 2009), General Foods, Sports Authority, Payless ShoeSource, Pebble smartwatches, TiVo. Each of their stories is different regarding the specific changes they were confronted with, but their outcomes were shared.[8] Those outcomes didn't care about the leaders' experience or beliefs or track record.

Disruption is inevitable. Either we can let it challenge our experiences and beliefs and inspire us to reshape them or we can dig in and fight from our comfort zones.

You have to be open to new ideas. You have to consider alternative futures. You have to look ahead. You have to challenge the status quo and your own ways of thinking. It's hard. But when you do the work to change your mindset, you become the captain of your own ship, and you can navigate through all the dangers of disruption and find a route to flourishing.

A Successful Mindshift Requires a Shift to a Beginner's Mind

A beginner's mind is characterized by intellectual openness, flexible thinking, and the capacity to consider new evidence against current beliefs.[9] You can see why it will be vital to mindshifting. Adopting a beginner's mind takes some practice, but the ways of practicing are lots of fun. One of them is to take a dive, however brief that might be, into stories from Eastern philosophy. The importance of a beginner's mind is a key tenant in these traditions.

Have you ever heard the story of the frog at the bottom of the well?

Jing Di Zhi Wa, or *The Frog at the Bottom of the Well*, is a popular Chinese fable from Zhuang Zi, an ancient book of anecdotes, allegories, and parables.[10] There are many interpretations of the story, but they each share a common moral: one's perspective in life is limited to what they know or choose to know.

In this story, the frog at the bottom of the well believes that the sky is only as big as the opening at the top. The frog's world and its worldly view are limited to the well itself. The frog knows nothing of the mountains, the seas and oceans, the trees, the flowers or plants, or the other lifeforms that inhabit the world outside of the well.

Dr. Daoshing Ni retells this fable this way:

Once upon a time, there lived a young frog at the bottom of a well. He had been there all his life and was very comfortable with his surroundings. As he looked up, he enjoyed his very small view of the sky. One day, his cousin came to visit from the outside world and asked the young frog why he had never ventured out of the well. The young frog replied, "I don't need to. I am quite comfortable here." Besides, the sky is so very small, there is nothing out there for me to see." His cousin pleaded with him for a long time and finally convinced the young frog to hop out of the well.

As he reached the midway point toward the top of the well, the young frog looked up and saw the sky broaden. He became fascinated and at the same time nervous and hesitant. His cousin continued to plead with him until he finally reached the top of the well. He was speechless as he gazed upon the vast sky in all directions. He could see trees and meadows and a beautiful pond. "I never knew how much beauty existed outside of the well," he exclaimed.[11]

The moral of the fable is that you should step outside of your comfort zone and look around. Only then will you be able to see the world of new opportunities emerging trends present. Only then can you perceive the world with a beginner's mind. This allows you to open your mind up to the emerging possibilities.

The term *beginner's mind* is a translation from a Japanese Zen term, "Shoshin" (初). Shoshin captures the spectacular paradox that the more you know, or think you know, about a subject, the more likely you are to close your mind to further learning, and the less likely you are to see and act upon novel solutions or opportunities.[12]

In Zen and Eastern philosophy, koans are used to combat this problem. Koans are stories designed to provoke "great doubt," test a student's progress in the Zen practice, and teach a complex lesson or meaning through a remarkably elementary story.[13] In one Zen koan, we can learn how a simple cup of tea can teach us how our thoughts prevent us from having an open mind.

The Story of a Simple Cup of Tea

Nan-in was a Japanese Zen master who lived during the Meiji era (1868–1912). One day, he was visited by a university professor who was curious about Zen. Nan-in served the professor a cup of tea. Rather than a traditional pour, Nan-in poured until the tea started to overflow. The professor could no longer watch as the tea spilled, saying to Nan-in, "It is overfull. No more will go in!"

Nan-in then turned to the professor and calmly explained, "Like the cup, you are too full of your own opinions and speculations. How can I show you Zen unless you first empty your cup?"[14]

In a separate interpretation of this popular Zen koan, the master stopped pouring, turned, and smiled at his guest. "You are like this teacup, so full that nothing more can be added. Come back to me when the cup is empty. Come back to me with an empty mind ready for filling."[15]

In this Zen koan, we learn that to learn we must first open our minds to learn something new and meaningful.

Learning a new skill or lesson requires unlearning those that prevent us from growing or even realizing that we can or need to grow. Emptying your cup and opening your mind is the first essential step toward a mindshift.

We tend not to see things as they are; we see them as *we* are.

But if we can teach ourselves to keep a more open mind, we could, at the very least, arrive at any given moment with a broader array of options or choices, which can result in supplemental possibilities and, ultimately, outcomes. To see the world with fresh eyes, one must be open to all possibilities, whether they align with your current trajectory or beliefs or not.

To learn about what it means to have a beginner's mind is to know a little about Shunryū Suzuki Roshi. He was one of the most famous "Soto Zen" monks of the 20th century. He moved to San Francisco in 1959 from Japan and gained popularity in the Western world for his unique way of teaching of Zen Buddhism.[16] Suzuki Roshi eventually established the Zen Center in San Francisco in 1962.[17] In 1970, Suzuki Roshi published what is largely regarded as a spiritual classic and one of the "most beloved of all American Zen books,"[18] *Zen Mind, Beginner's Mind*.[19]

Though *Zen Mind, Beginner's Mind* was his one and only book, it still endures today, "treasured for its beautiful expression and life-changing insights."[20]

The book's premise reflects Suzuki Roshi's teachings to live life with a pure mind, one open to possibilities:

> "If your mind is empty, it is always ready for anything; it is open to everything. In the beginner's mind there are many possibilities; in the expert's mind there are few."[21]

That profound sentence is referenced countless times. It is sourced from a lecture Suzuki Roshi gave in November 1965. During the development of the book, Trudy Dixon, a close disciple of Suzuki Roshi, took on the editing job shortly before her passing. It is her work that refined the words we know today.

At surface level, it seems simple enough. An open mind sees opportunities that the expert's mind might miss. The expert's mind is the hammer Maslow spoke of, and our own biases prevent us from seeing hidden gems or recognizing the nuances in the details around us. Suzuki Roshi isn't saying, however, that becoming an expert is something we shouldn't strive to achieve. He isn't purporting that we shouldn't gather skill, knowledge, or experience. Instead, he warns us that our knowledge can get in the way of us seeing something in its own essence for its true potential.

Interestingly, another of the world's great thinkers, from the Western tradition, also warned about the expert's mind. Italian Christian theologian and philosopher St. Thomas Aquinas once warned, "Beware of the man with one book."[22] His meaning in these words was based in the context of debate. If someone has become an absolute expert in one topic or field, studying or writing just one book, they will undoubtedly out-debate you on the subject. But this is also their limitation when it comes to changes in their field that they may not see. It affects their ability to see beyond the dogma that has defined their life and work because their purview and perspective are limited to their "one book."

So, to attain a beginner's mind, start by accepting that as much as you may know, there's so much more you don't.

The next step is to open your mind, which begins with admitting that your mind is not open, yet.

Our Minds Like to Close On Us

Suzuki Roshi said, "The true purpose [of Zen] is to see things as they are, to observe things as they are, and to let everything go as it goes ... Zen practice is to open up our small mind."[23]

A closed-minded person doesn't question their own beliefs or perspectives.[24] We've all encountered some of them. Recognizing closed-mindedness in others is far easier than recognizing it in ourselves. And we are all guilty of closing our minds, whether intentionally or not. One simple test to see if you're closed-minded —or at least somewhat closed-minded —is whether you can listen to an opposing view before you start forming a counterargument in your mind.

Achieving a beginner's mind is challenging because we've learned, unintentionally, to close our minds, at least about some things. We've grown up, from home to school to church to work to everything in between, learning how to think, following the rules, never to speak out of turn or question elders or experts. We operate in a safe zone, or what we think is a safe zone.

But ask yourself, do you want to be guilty of rejecting new possibilities in the way most people did in these cases:

German geophysicist Alfred Wegener proposed in 1912 that Earth was made up of shifting continental plates only to be ridiculed by "expert" geologists around the world. Wegener's "delirious ravings" were likened to pseudoscience because they went against the popular conventions of the time. It would take decades before the accuracy of his theory would be proven.[25]

Neuroscientist Santiago Ramón y Cajal's "harsh decree" supposed that adult humans were unable to grow new neurons. Until the 1990s, neurologists based their practice on these doctrines, which were, if you can imagine today's world, established in the late 19th to early 20th century. This dogma lasted so long that it affected the progress of neurobiology. In fact, the work between the early 1960s and 1990s was deemed "heretical" until the neurogenesis in the adult brain could no longer be denied.[26]

When COVID-19 shut the world down in 2020, a study that examined data collected from 17 countries found evidence that closed-minded people were less likely to adhere to preventive behaviors, such as physical distancing and wearing masks.[27] What's worse, they participated in the spread of misinformation to justify their position, putting others at risk while claiming to be superior to those who were open to following recommendations and guidelines.

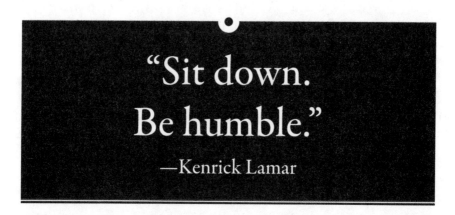

"Sit down.
Be humble."
—Kenrick Lamar

Overcoming the Pitfalls of Intellectual Hubris

When we bring an "I know" mindset, we block curiosity and imagination. And since these are important precursors to creativity and innovation, we can't see things differently or actually explore new horizons. We remain in the same box we're trying to think outside of.

We each, in our own way, possess an "expert's mind." And in many ways, we also go through each day with a closed mind. The key is to willfully open it, to practice a beginner's mind as often as we can, to see differently, and to respond with a more open, positive, and beneficial impact.

Christian Jarrett, deputy editor of *Psyche*, described in great lengths how cultivating a beginner's mind helps to rediscover the joy of learning.

> People who are more intellectually humble actually know more, presumably because they are more receptive to new information. Similarly, being intellectually humble is associated with open-mindedness and a greater willingness to be receptive to other people's perspectives—arguably just the tonic that our politically febrile world needs today.[28]

Research backs this up. Five studies examined how intellectual humility relates to acquiring knowledge and learning. Published in 2019, the paper "Links Between Intellectual Humility and Acquiring Knowledge" found that closed minds tend to distort information to fit their beliefs.[29] This can then affect their interpretation of information and the extent to which they acquire knowledge. Intellectual humility, on the other hand, is conceptualized as a trait and a virtue, meaning it is a distinguishing quality and reflective of behavior relevant to gaining new knowledge. Simply stated, to truly learn, one must possess the humility necessary to realize that they have something to learn.

Intellectually humble people are not threatened by intellectual disagreements. They're not overconfident about their knowledge. They respect others' points of view. And they are open to revising their viewpoints when warranted.[30] Intellectually humble people understand and accept that they are not perfect and that there may be faults in their perspectives. This works to counter our own biases in that intellectual humility protects us from uncritically accepting our perspectives as accurate. Instead, we can possess an openness to new information to improve our current knowledge.

A beginner's mind asks the "me" or "I" or the ego to take a step, or more, back. Not only is this vital to seeing the possibilities of emerging trends we might be tempted to naysay, but it's essential to adopting a growth mindset, which as we'll explore next, is another component of the ability to mindshift.

Chapter 5

The Growth Mindmap: It's All in Your Mind...Set

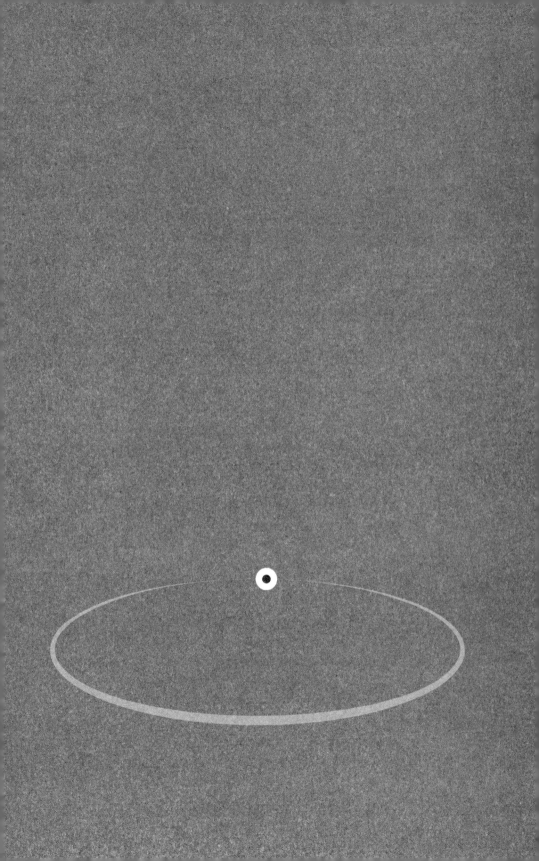

> ## "Go to bed smarter than when you woke up."
> —Charlie Munger

Stanford professor Carol S. Dweck has won numerous awards for her research, including her groundbreaking work in identifying two important mindsets, *growth* and *fixed*, that determine our ability to learn and flourish or face a more difficult time in growing beyond where we are today. Those with growth mindsets, she learned, believe their abilities can be developed. Those with fixed mindsets believe their abilities are carved in stone.[1]

Dr. Dweck's findings are based on in-depth research that studied students' attitudes about failure. Her team observed that some students rebound after experiencing setbacks, large and small, while others are devastated. When students believe they can get smarter, they invest in the effort to do so, which also makes them stronger and more resilient. As a result, they put in extra time and effort, which contributes to higher achievement.[2]

In *Mindset: The New Psychology of Success*, Dr. Dweck posits, "What are the consequences of thinking that your intelligence or personality is something you can develop, as opposed to something that is a fixed, deep-seated trait?"

In her book,[3] Dr. Dweck explains that those with fixed mindsets are constantly seeking validation to prove their worth not just to others, but also to themselves.[4]

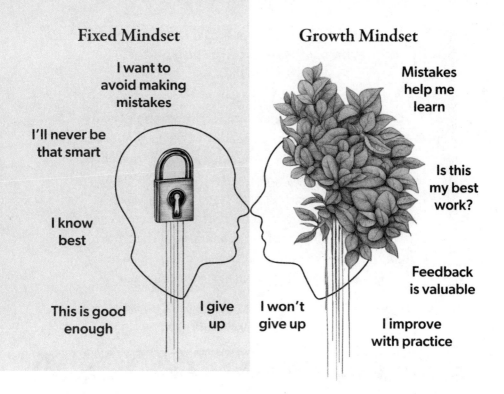

Fixed Mindset

I want to
avoid making
mistakes

I'll never be
that smart

I know
best

This is good
enough

I give
up

Growth Mindset

Mistakes
help me
learn

Is this
my best
work?

Feedback
is valuable

I won't
give up

I improve
with practice

Dweck writes:

> "I've seen so many people with this one consuming
> goal of proving themselves in the classroom, in their
> careers, and in their relationships. Every situation calls
> for a confirmation of their intelligence, personality, or
> character. Every situation is evaluated: Will I succeed or
> fail? Will I look smart or dumb? Will I be accepted or
> rejected? Will I feel like a winner or a loser?"

On the other hand, those with growth mindsets are driven
by a desire to learn and grow. They have a tendency to embrace
challenges, persist in the face of setbacks, see effort as a path
to mastery, learn from criticism and feedback, and find lessons
and inspiration from the success of others. Those with a growth
mindset, Dweck writes, see "the hand you're dealt is just the
starting point for development. This growth mindset is based on
the belief that your basic qualities are things you can cultivate
through your efforts."

"Why waste time proving over and over how great you are," Dweck writes, **"when you could be getting better?"**

Dweck continues:

> Why hide deficiencies instead of overcoming them? Why look for friends or partners who will just shore up your self-esteem instead of ones who will also challenge you to grow? And why seek out the tried and true, instead of experiences that will stretch you? The passion for stretching yourself and sticking to it, even (or especially) when it's not going well, is the hallmark of the growth mindset. This is the mindset that allows people to thrive during some of the most challenging times in their lives.

How do these mindsets differ, specifically? The following are some examples of fixed versus growth mindsets:

Fixed Mindset	Growth Mindset
Either I am good at it or I'm not.	I can learn anything I want.
That's just who I am.	I am constantly evolving, a work in progress.
If you have to work hard, you don't have the ability.	The more you challenge yourself, the smarter you become.
If I don't try something new, I won't fail at it.	I only fail when I stop trying.
That job or relationship or thing is out of my league.	It is challenging, but I'm going after it.

Do you believe you can, and want to, learn and grow? Or do you make excuses and assess blame? Legendary basketball coach John Wooden once said that no one is a failure until they start blaming others.[5]

> "...in the growth mindset, failure can be a painful experience. But it doesn't define you. It's a problem to be faced, dealt with, and learned from."[6]

While you can't control the events that happen around or to you, you can control how you respond to them.

Those who possess a growth mindset aren't necessarily born with it. Dweck has found that some cultivate it. You can too.

In a world that is wrestling with reimagining what's possible, a growth mindset is essential for achieving a mindshift. A fixed mindset is going to do its best to make tomorrow look a lot like yesterday.

Fixed Mindset
Abilities bound to limitations

Vicious Cycle

All of this confirms...

PERSPECTIVE
Life is a test.
Do what you know.
Avoid making mistakes.
Surround yourself with
like-minded people.

**Feedback loops foster
confirmation bias, status quo bias,
confidence bias, among others.**

HORIZON
The future is uncertain.
The unknown = fear.
New normal =
evolved business as usual.

**Success measures are
tied to legacy models.**

NEW EXPERIENCES
Inputs reinforce existing beliefs.
Leaders possess overconfidence bias.
New ideas = potential threats
which limit experimentation.

OPPORTUNITIES
Risk averse.
New opportunities are limited to
prevailing mindsets and
mental models.

**Failure is limited to "safe"
investments. Short-termism
drives investment threshold
and potential.**

CAPABILITIES
Skillsets are focused
on optimizing existing models.
New skillsets are limited to iteration,
confusing it with innovation.

**Understand customers
only as data, by silo. Not
customer-centered,
instead company-centered.**

Virtuous Cycle

Growth Mindset
Abilities evolve through plasticity

 PERSPECTIVE
Life is a journey of learning.
Seek people who challenge you.
Intentionally collaborate with
different people.

All of this confirms...

 HORIZON
The future is uncertain, so what?
Learn to activate a receiver's state to
unlock input to new signals.
The next normal is TBD (by you).

**Feedback loops
foster colearning and
ideation for continuous
improvement and growth.**

 NEW EXPERIENCES
Signals open minds to new
possibilities and areas to grow.
Receivers collect signals to interpret
as trends (threats + opportunities).

**Growth optimizes legacy and
also creates new business
and operating models.**

 OPPORTUNITIES
Appetite for risk increases.
New opportunities are hunted,
understood, and developed.
Growth leadership sets the
tone for a growth culture.

**Long-termism: A founder's edge
connects vision to "Test & Learn"
initiatives in iteration and innovation.
Failure = measured progress.
Success = adaptation.**

 CAPABILITIES
New skillsets tied to opportunities.
Learning becomes continuous.
Unlocks new experiences
and growth.
Creates a sense of comfort and
control through uncertaintly.

**Leaders are driven by digital
empathy (humanized 360°
customer data) and inspired
by new customer behaviors
and expectations.**

Fixed Mindset: Vicious Cycle

A growth mindset leads to a "virtuous cycle of beliefs and behaviors." A fixed mindset leads to an equally powerful "vicious cycle" that discourages or belittles growth thinking and action.

In the **vicious cycle**, those with fixed mindsets believe that their abilities are immutable or unchangeable.

 Perspective: Life is a test. Do what you know. Avoid making mistakes. Surround yourself with like-minded people. Defend the fiefdom. Limit diversity and inclusion. Fear uncertainty.

 Horizon: The future is uncertain, and uncertainty is linked to the unknown, which is also indicative of fear. This leads to behaviors that tend to avoid new experiences or inputs. Default behaviors seek to connect the dots between normal and the next normal because it is what fixed mindsets know. When you don't know what you don't know, there is an illusion of certainty to it.

 Newish experiences: New inputs that do not reinforce our beliefs and values represent the unknown and do not apply to existing frameworks or metrics systems. They are to be avoided with an abundance of caution. These leaders believe they have the experience necessary to keep growing. Anything that challenges their experience and expertise, or models, is considered a potential threat.

 Opportunities: Breaking out of routines is a slow, cumbersome, and often political and exhausting process. Everything is by committee. Even though new opportunities represent real promise because of market shifts, every investment is always reviewed through a cost-center lens. Changes in patterns, routines, and behaviors along with emerging trends are minimized, overlooked, or trivialized because of the absence of a beginner's mind, curiosity, and purposeful understanding. New investments reinforce prevailing mindsets and mental models lead to iteration, the improvement of yesterday's performance using new technologies and optimized processes.

 Risk: The key words here are risk averse. It's the same mentality that battens down the hatches and cuts costs during more "uncertain" times and events. The process for exploring new investment opportunities is considered after other perceived priorities are examined. It's the proverbial "Why fix something if it ain't broke?" Any investment in something new is weighed as elements of risk and cost versus risk and reward. Where possibility lies in terms of innovation, risk will always outweigh promise, and thus returns are limited accordingly. Everything is mitigated through analysis and comparisons to competition. But they miss what's happening on the edges where startups and innovators are exploring and adapting to opportunities others miss.

 Capabilities: Legacy-based skillsets are narrow (or focused) by design. These leaders believe they got to where they are for good reason. They are in their positions for good reason. Their ability to adapt to change is to try to stuff the pegs, regardless of shape, into the same hole, filling the same box, to protect business as usual. It's akin to the adage "When you're a hammer, everything looks like a nail." Any new skillsets required as technology and markets evolve will be aimed at scaling business as usual, making it faster and more efficient, and exploring opportunities for increased margins.

 Customers/stakeholders: True customer-centricity or empathy is absent. Understanding is tied only to data, not people, and that data is siloed by function. A complete 360 view is impossible. Decision-makers are not customers or stakeholders. Decisions and consequently outcomes are focused on business parameters and not on customer or stakeholder impact. Fixed mindsets are company-centric, not customer-centric, prioritizing short-termism in the name of shareholder and leadership value—first, but not solely.

Test and learn: Failure is a threshold. It's limited through "safe" and intermittent investments. But their success is hindered out of the gate because new programs are bound and measured by fixed models. Success measures are tied to legacy models.

 Feedback loop: Signals and inputs are driven by stakeholders, shareholders, the board, et al., with measures driven by the interests of all respective parties. Feedback is limited to groupthink, validating mindsets, and preserving the status quo.

Thus, the vicious cycle repeats itself, until it runs its course and loses momentum and begins a downward spiral.

In the **virtuous cycle**, those with growth mindsets believe that their abilities are malleable. Dr. Dweck refers to the connection between a growth mindset and neuroplasticity, your brain's ability to change and grow over time when exposed to learning new things.[7] This is a topic I explored in depth in my book, *Lifescale: How to Live a More Creative, Productive, and Happy Life*. The premise was based on changing one's daily digital behaviors and habits to rewire the brain away from multitasking and distractions toward single-tasking and focus (to achieve flow).

 Perspective: Life is a journey of learning. Surround yourself with people who challenge and teach you. Intentionally explore how to collaborate with different people and teams. Contribute to a more open, diverse, and inclusive culture. Embrace uncertainty and learn how to thrive in new situations. Don't worry about not knowing what to do; just be resilient.

 Horizon: Seek new experiences and inputs to better understand the unknown. Appreciate business as usual and normal for its known attributes and deliverables, meaning identify best practices. Learn how to activate and sharpen your receiver's state to receive signals that indicate potential trends, threats, and new opportunities.

New experiences: The sharper the receiver's state, the clearer the signals become to see new trends, opportunities, and looming disruptions. Here, leaders become open to allow new inputs, challenges, beliefs, and values. They ask questions like, What does this mean? What do we need to think about to maximize this opportunity or not be disrupted by it? It creates a persistent cycle of openness, adapting, and improving. This leads to ideation and the development of new programs or pilots that enhance existing frameworks and metrics for success.

Opportunities: A beginner's mind sees ways to iterate and innovate, specifically. Improving and enhancing existing processes and models represents one path. Visionaries connect the dots to ideas that can also unlock new possibilities. Growth-minded leadership is now necessary to operate efforts in iteration and innovation in parallel. Teams then learn how to work differently, and differently together, moving in the same direction according to the vision. Boards, advisors, and stakeholders must all be brought in. Corporate culture must be reimagined in alignment with a thoughtful, well-articulated vision.

Risk: A culture of risk-taking increases the appetite for venturing into the unknown and is the only path toward strategic innovation and growth. You don't just grow because you do more of the same thing, aka better sameness. You ideate, test, learn, and grow where it makes sense. The process for exploring new investment opportunities is evaluated in parallel. Any investment in something new is weighed as elements of risk and reward versus risk and cost. Appetite for risk isn't greater because of a betting mentality, but instead as measured and thoughtful explorations in growth. The basis for risk isn't solely compared to competitors but also to those leaders on the edges who are unlocking new opportunities. Risk and innovation become ingredients in a growth culture.

Capabilities: The delta between ideas and opportunities forms the roadmap for the tools, resources, and skillsets necessary to venture into these new frontiers. New opportunities require new skillsets and the bridge to mastering the unknown. It creates comfort in learning and applying new skills that put the work into moving in new directions and unlocking new experiences and growth. This then feeds the part of the organization that can scale new skills and outputs through efficiencies and automation. That pursuit of growth, though, is the ongoing counterbalance.

Customers/stakeholders: Empathetic leaders create "customer companies" by aiming to understand customers (and employees) better. Data and insights focus on surfacing "digital empathy" and the human side of behaviors, expectations, preferences, and changes. This provides a 360° view of the customer and their evolving preferences and expectations. These insights influence growth opportunities for the short- and long-term, splitting investments into ways to improve experiences and services, through new tech, processes, and policies today, and explore ways to align with trends to better do so over time.

Test and learn: A visionary leader can articulate opportunities. A visionary leader must also drive and/ or fully support testing and learning as part of a culture of innovation. Visionary leaders either possess a founder's edge or surround themselves with those who possess a founder's edge. They execute, drive, measure, adapt, and learn. Failure is an expected part of the learning process. Here, failure loses its traditional negative connotations and indicates steps toward success. It's a measure of progress. The only failure here is not trying at all. To succeed in new areas, you have to keep trying. Testing and learning improve existing models and also create new value through new models, the growth balance between iteration and innovation.

Feedback loop: Growth mindsets believe that skills and mindsets can always improve; 360°, productive feedback becomes important to the growth process. A growth culture is nurtured through testing and learning. Learning is shaped by feedback loops that measure progress in iteration and innovation efforts. Insights are shared across and up the organization to communicate progress, identify learning opportunities, and create alignment in new endeavors. Growth mindsets continue to be curious, ask questions, focus on areas for development, accept challenges, and pursue learning opportunities.[8] New ideas to iterate and innovate become productive and abundant to drive continuous improvement and growth.

Futures mindset: *This does not include the vicious cycle, because it's not a common practice in organizations where leaders possess fixed mindsets.* The next stage in growth is one that actively looks to the future to plan for present actions and investments in growth.

Thus, the virtuous cycle repeats itself, with the aim of unlocking new opportunities.

How to Foster a Growth Mindset

You start by opening your mind to

different **circumstances**,

different **inputs**,

different **ways forward**,

different **people around you**,

and different **feedback based on your newfound mindset**.

Soon enough you'll find yourself more open and curious, with a newfound ability to

- ✅ feel empathy,
- ✅ see problems in a new light,
- ✅ see new opportunities,
- ✅ pay attention to unforeseen trends,
- ✅ listen to new voices,
- ✅ discover uncharted paths,
- ✅ do the things you didn't expect were possible,
- ✅ and inspire others to follow, align, plug in, and join in their own way.

All the while you change your trajectory and the trajectory of those around you.

To connect a beginner's mind toward a growth mindset, start by believing that you can. Then take the next steps, step-by-step, to perceive events more openly, broaden your horizons, explore new ways to unlearn and learn, and believe in yourself and those around you. This is how you make the mindshift from a fixed to a growth mindset and beyond.

Accept uncertainty.

Remember, focus on what you can control. Uncertainty is just a reality, a way of life. In this zeitgeist, the more we try to bring the past forward, the more likely we are to destabilize our future.

Cultivate your sense of purpose.

People with a growth mindset have a greater sense of purpose—a reason for what they're doing, where they're going, and why.[9] This keeps them centered and focused on what matters…

learning, unlearning, betterment, growth. And it keeps them asking "why" and applying their curiosity and learnings to the meaning of their work. They may even turn it into the spark that also becomes their passion. Once they find it, they embrace it. Their purpose will evolve and grow as they go.

Stay curious and always be learning (ABL).

Keep that beginner's mind clear, open, and ready. These are novel times, and there's much to learn to blaze new trails. But as you go, that beginner's mind will keep you curious and keep you open to discovery, which will help keep you learning.

Build incremental momentum.

Plan for incremental success and appreciate your progress.[10] Assess where you may exhibit fixed mindset behaviors and learn how to address them. Give your transformation a sense of purpose. Where are there opportunities to learn or do something different? What are the trends that you can better understand? What are the skills you can learn to do the jobs of tomorrow? Figure this out and then take steps toward learning something new or unlearning something that's holding you back, every day.

Embrace the idea of failure.

"The one who falls and gets up is stronger than the one who never tried. Do not fear failure but rather fear not trying."[11] These are the words of Roy T. Bennett, and they inspire us to rethink the meaning of the word failure from unsuccessful or incapable to trying and learning and trying again. Venturing into unknown territory has no standard for success, yet. It's failure only if you give up or believe you have nothing to learn.

Find the courage to persist.

Setbacks happen. Growth happens when you allow that spark within you to burn brighter and brighter. Stoke it. This is courage. Unleash that inner boldness and the strength to grow in the face of uncertainty. This is what separates true leaders from everyone else. Dr. Dweck characterized how those with growth mindsets respond to setbacks, "The other thing exceptional people seem to have is a special talent for converting life's setbacks into future successes."[12]

Embrace the promise of "yet."

In her TED talk, Dr. Dweck described two ways to think about problems that seem just out of your reach for solving, those outside of your comfort zone. A growth mindset will lean into this challenge accepting that while you do not yet have an answer, the key is that you've not solved it—yet. Fixed mindsets will run away from or fight against difficulty. Growth mindsets are driven by possibilities, with the idea that they can learn their way toward resolution.[13] You'll learn to engage deeply. You'll figure it out.

Reflect on your progress.

Reflect on your progress. With a growth mindset comes growth. It only matters when you see and appreciate the steps you're taking and in which ways you're growing. Take time to look at your previous state, current state, and incremental improvements as you progress. This becomes part of your narrative.

Don't give an F.

Don't give an F. No one will remember your failures, but everyone will remember your success. And if they do hang on solely to the times you fall, without regard for the number of times you kept getting back up, forget them. Seriously.

Chapter 6

The Wonder of Awe

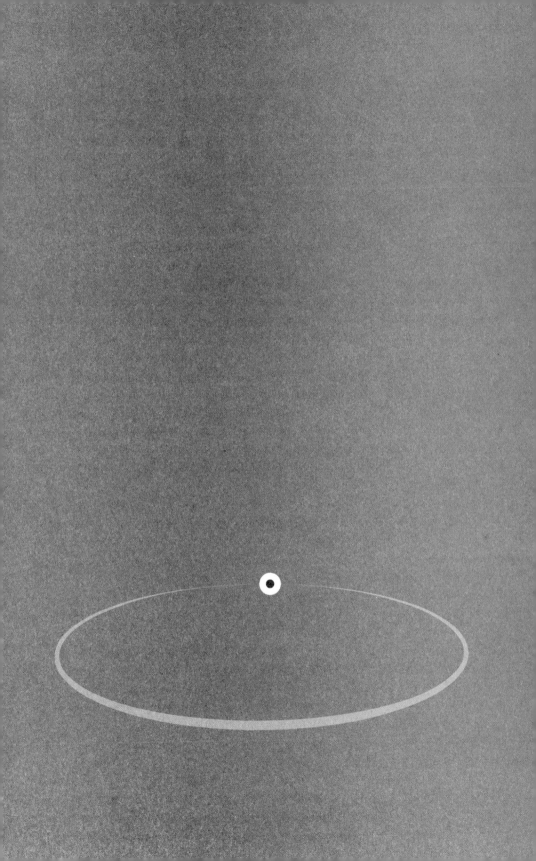

"The world is full of magical things — patiently waiting for our senses to grow sharper."

—W.B. Yeats

Won·der *verb*
The desire to be curious to know something; to think about things in a questioning and sometimes doubting way.[1]

Won·der *noun*
A feeling of amazement and admiration, caused by something beautiful, remarkable, or unfamiliar."

Have

you visited a foreign country or city and found yourself wandering without a destination as you marveled at landscapes and architectures? As I travel the world for work, I make sure to take time, whenever it is, even though I really never have the time. I just make the space for it to happen. I'm fully present in those moments. Though I have pictures of every place I've visited, my favorite images are those forever emblazoned in my brain.

Or have you ever sat on a beach or in a park or taken a walk at night just to gaze at the stars, with no other plans than to marvel at their shimmering brilliance?

I am lucky enough to spend time in the Sierras surrounding North Lake Tahoe in Nevada. No matter the temperature outside, no matter the season, I will often take time to pause and stare into space to marvel at just how brightly the rich field of stars shine above.

Where I live, there aren't many streetlights or buildings, which makes light pollution nonexistent. On a clear night, it's just you and the stars, a shower of light and hope that surrounds you, making you believe it's just for you. And when a full moon rises, you hold your breath for a moment, your eyes open wider, your heart beats a little slower, and your soul glows a little brighter.

When you slow the clock enough, block out distractions, and zoom in, you are awestruck every time.

The same is true for beach sunsets. I'm a sucker for sunsets and chase them as often as I can. There's something about that slow, then fast, dive of a glowing orange sphere into the vastness of blue. And then comes my favorite part…magic hour. It's a bonus time to enjoy the last moments of sunlight while basking in and embracing the orange and blue glow.

I call the feeling of these moments "the wonder of awe." They never get old, and I never can get enough of them.

Feeling this incredible emotion of awe doesn't require witnessing a grand act of nature. Awe can be triggered by anything, anywhere, if you're open to it.

Thinking Like a Child Is AWEsome and Will Make You an AWEsome Leader, Too

To experience awe is to think like a child.

Mencius, a Chinese Confucian philosopher who was regarded as the "second Sage" to Confucius himself, once said, to paraphrase, that a wise person is one who doesn't lose the child's heart and mind.[2]

Just think for a minute about the most common questions kids ask.[3]

Why does it rain?

Why does our neighbor look different?

Where do babies come from?

How do airplanes fly?

Who made the sun and moon?

Why does it snow?

Why is the sky blue?

How much salt is in the ocean?

How do birds fly?

Why do I have to go to school?

Why do I need to eat vegetables?

How are babies made?

Why? Why? Why?

Oftentimes, the questions can become too much.

"It just is!"

"Stop asking!"

"Because!"

But we must not extinguish their little fires of wonder. As children ask questions, they learn, their brains start to grow and mature, their synapses are expanding, and their analytical skills improve.

Asking questions at a young age does the following:

| Stimulates their little brains | Helps them overcome anxiety | Encourages interpersonal relationships | Increases interest in reading | Improves communication skills |

The same was once true for us.

Our inquisitive and imaginative young minds were ceaselessly fascinated by the world around us. Professor Frank C. Keil is the director of the Cognition and Development Lab at Yale University. He wrote a piece for Literary Hub in 2022 titled "Where Does Childhood Wonder Come From—And Why Does It End?" He wrote, "We are all born with many essential ingredients of wonder—with inquisitive minds, fascinated by the world around us." But at some point in our lives, usually before or by the end of our teenage school years, the powers of curiosity and wonder lose their strengths. "Almost anywhere one looks, children seem to have a hunger for scientific explanations and adults have little appetite if any," Keil continued.

We lose our ability to see life as a magical fountain of newness. "The consequences of this loss of wonder are profound," Keil remarked. "Abandonment of wonder deprives us of the intensely rewarding joy of discovery."

Influential marine biologist, writer, and conservationist Rachel Carson, published many works in addition to the one she's best known for, *Silent Spring*. In *The Sense of Wonder*, she wrote[4]:

> "A child's world is fresh and new and beautiful, full of wonder and excitement. It is our misfortune that for most of us that clear-eyed vision, that true instinct for what is beautiful and awe-inspiring, is dimmed and even lost before we reach adulthood. If I had influence with the good fairy who is supposed to preside over all children, I should ask that her gift to each child in the world be a sense of wonder so indestructible that it would last throughout life."

But the loss of wonder is not inevitable. In his 2007 bestseller, *Einstein: His Life and Universe*, Walter Isaacson wrote of the loveable genius:

> "He never lost his sense of wonder at the magic of nature's phenomena—magnetic fields, gravity, inertia, acceleration, light beams—which grown-ups find so commonplace."[5]

As Einstein's astonishing out-of-the-box—well, out-of-the-galaxy—thinking suggests, that rekindling of our sense of wonder, experiencing awe, can lead to great discoveries. Research finds that, among adults, awe can also promote humility, stimulate learning, increase perceptions of uncertainty, diminish personal concerns, reduce dogmatism, and increase perceptions of social cohesion.[6] What's not to love?

Reigniting our sense of wonder is actually easy. It just takes being mindful that we can find awe-inspiring experiences all around us. For example, when you order your favorite dish or watch your favorite movie or listen to your favorite song or visit your favorite destination, whatever it is, you should see, taste, smell, hear, or feel it again for the first time. Let go of expectations. Be present in the moment. Savor it. Try to notice something different. Find a new way to be grateful for it in your life. Mary Davis, author of the beloved classic *Every Day Spirit*, famously observed, "The more grateful I am, the more beauty I see."[7]

The more we find ways to experience wonder, the more we will also stimulate our curiosity. Frank Keil highlights that "Childlike wonder results in an overwhelming sense of curiosity. This sense of curiosity makes innovative people constantly ask 'why' and 'what if' questions." Here again, we can take a cue from Albert Einstein. Late in his life, he wrote to a friend about the importance of stoking the powers of childlike wonder. "People like you and me never grow old. We never cease to stand like curious children before the great mystery into which we were born."[8]

Einstein believed curiosity is one of humanity's best traits. "The important thing is not to stop questioning," he counseled in 1955. "Curiosity has its own reason for existing. One cannot help but be in awe when he contemplates the mysteries of eternity, of life, of the marvelous structure of reality. It is enough if one tries merely to comprehend a little of this mystery each day. Never lose a holy curiosity."[9]

There are so many benefits we get from curiosity, some of which are surprising. Author Samantha Green has studied research on curiosity, and she elaborates some of its benefits. "A curious person is better able to handle unwanted emotions or thoughts, as they are simply the start to questions and new discoveries," she wrote. She continued, "A curious person is also more likely to seek out the new, and is more accepting of conflict between what they know and contradictory information."[10]

This makes me think of one of my favorite scenes from the hit series *Ted Lasso*, about the value of curiosity.

What Ted Lasso Can Teach Us About Curiosity

If you haven't watched the series *Ted Lasso*, I highly recommend it. Jason Sudeikis stars as an American college football coach who is hired to turn around a major Premiership football (soccer to my American friends) team in England: AFC Richmond. I don't want to ruin the story for you, so I'll simply say that Coach Lasso doesn't have any experience with, or knowledge about, football/soccer. The reason he's hired for a job he's unqualified to perform is essential to the story arc. It's a lovable series of lessons in being human when you're a fish out of water.

While it's a series about sports, the show itself is a very special stage for *Ted Lasso*'s magical recipe of kindness, hope, and optimism. Each episode teaches us to believe in ourselves and each other, explore more meaningful friendships and relationships, and, most of all, kill everyone with kindness and resolve to win games and win over even the harshest of critics and cynics.

One of my favorite scenes takes place in the eighth episode of the first season.[11]

At the time, the main antagonist of the story is Rupert, the former owner of the team Ted Lasso now coaches. Rupert is also the ex-husband of Rebecca, who is the new owner of the team following their divorce. Let's just say he's vindictive, unwilling to let go of the team in spirit, and making it extremely difficult for the team's hopes of success. I'll let you describe his character after you watch the show.

In one scene, Rupert disrespects Rebecca in a pub, The Crown and Anchor, that also serves as the HQ for local AFC Richmond fans. This crude act is done in front of Coach Lasso, his team of coaches and players, and his fans. At this moment in the series, it's just the latest example of Rupert's ongoing harassment.

Coach Lasso takes the moment to do the right thing and stand up for Rebecca's honor by calmly walking over to the dartboard where Rupert is standing and strategically provoking him into a gentleman's wager over darts.

Coach Lasso picks up a dart with his right hand and throws it at the board, hitting nothing of significance.

Rupert asks Coach Lasso if he plays darts and then challenges him to a game with a wager of £10,000. Lasso admits that playing for that kind of money is too rich for his blood, so he proposes an alternative wager.

If Rupert wins, he will pick the starting lineup for the last two games. If Coach Lasso wins, Rupert must stay away from the owner's box while Rebecca is in charge. Rupert, with great pride and an inflated ego, willfully accepts the challenge, pulling his own personal set of darts from his pocket and sarcastically realizing out loud, "Oh, I forgot I had these on me."

To which, Lasso quips, "Oh wait, I forgot I'm left-handed." He then throws the dart, with his left hand, directly at the bullseye.

What happens next is a masterclass in leadership, humility, character, and how to "be curious and not judgmental."

As we approach the final moments of the game, it's clear that Rupert is in the lead. To those watching, though, it's not evident if Rupert is the better player or if Lasso is hustling Rupert. It *is* clear to Rupert, however, that he is not only the better player; he's already claiming victory before the match is over. But then...

As Lasso picks up another dart, he shares with Rupert that people have underestimated him since he was a child. He says that really bothered him, but then one day, when he was taking his son to school, he saw a Walt Whitman quote on a wall: "Be curious, not judgmental." At that, he throws another bullseye. And proceeds to keep hitting the points necessary to win.

After he wins the game, he points out to Rupert how important it is to ask questions and to be curious; ask questions like "Have you played a lot of darts, Ted?" Turns out that Lasso had played every Sunday with his father at a sports bar when he was a kid. It's a reminder that, though it's hard to see, we are not the center of the universe.

Transcending Awe to Self-Transcendence

Another great value of rekindling our sense of wonder is that the awe it will lead us to feel is a conduit to self-transcendence. Awe-struck people become less self-centered and rise above the self. Once someone experiences awe, they are more likely to think about the future in their decisions and actions, contemplate consequences of their behaviors, and pay more attention to the needs and interests of others.[12]

Self-transcendence brings the individual what Abraham Maslow termed *peak experiences*, in which they transcend their own personal concerns and see from a higher perspective. Maslow described peak experiences as "rare, exciting, oceanic, deeply moving, exhilarating, elevating experiences that generate an advanced form of perceiving reality and are even mystic and magical in their effect upon the experimenter."[13]

These experiences often release positive emotions like joy, peace, and a well-developed sense of awareness, which are core to a beginner's mind and fundamental to mindshift.[14]

The connection between awe and a beginner's mind is to set the stage for opening one's mind, readying it to receive, appreciate, and seek to understand and act upon important life signals and build upon them in our lives.

Maslow further described peak experiences as:

> "feelings of limitless horizons opening up to the vision, the feeling of being simultaneously more powerful and also more helpless than one ever was before, the feeling of great ecstasy and wonder and awe, the loss of placing in time and space with, finally, the conviction that something extremely important and valuable had happened, so that the subject is to some extent transformed and strengthened even in his daily life by such experiences."[15]

Maslow linked peak experiences as the catalyst to self-transcendence. The following happens when an individual experiences awe:

It transcends their own identity,

causes a shift in perception,

triggers curiosity,

creates a new opening or expands one's mind,

ignites imagination and helps one see things in a new way,

inspires one to become part of something larger than ourselves,

sparks a desire to connect with others,[16]

and may be linked to a willingness to take more risks and find levels of comfort with uncertainty.[17]

I'm sure you've seen the famous pyramid that depicts Maslow's model. The Hierarchy of Needs was first introduced in 1943, described in his paper "A Theory of Human Motivation," published in *Psychological Review*.[18] Maslow introduced this model to understand the motivations for human behavior.[19] He believed that people who sought to better themselves needed to mostly obtain the needs in lower levels before they could realize upper levels, where self-actualization was placed at the very top, representing our fullest potential as humans.

Here's a fun fact: though Maslow's Hierarchy of Needs is visualized as an iconic pyramid, he never organized his model as such.[20] Maslow did not view his hierarchy as a series of levels, where the journey reaches the top of one level to unlock the next, and so on. Not everyone has the same needs arranged and initialized in the same order. In his writing, Maslow believed that we are not solely motivated to pursue or achieve one need at a time; instead, we continuously go back and forth with some needs partially satisfied and partially unsatisfied. We can and do aim for multiple needs at one time.

Here's another fun fact: though self-actualization is represented as the pinnacle of Maslow's Hierarchy of Needs, he didn't believe that it was the pinnacle of human development in the end.[21] Instead, he later realized that self-transcendence, above oneself, was the true pinnacle.

Maslow described transcendence this way:

> "Transcendence refers to the very highest and most inclusive or holistic levels of human consciousness, behaving and relating, as ends rather than means, to oneself, to significant others, to human beings in general, to other species, to nature, and to the cosmos."[22]

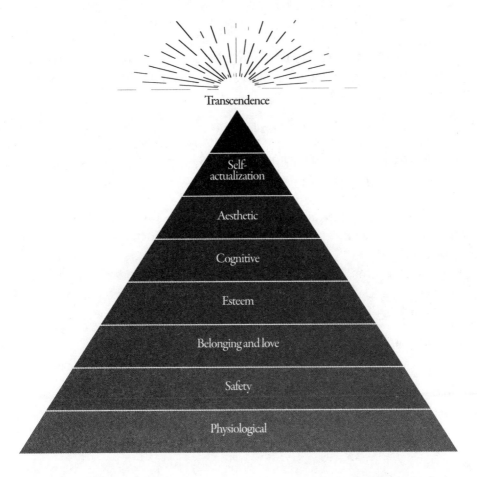

Transcendence

Self-actualization

Aesthetic

Cognitive

Esteem

Belonging and love

Safety

Physiological

In simpler terms, self-transcendence is about rising above oneself and appreciating and connecting to that which is greater than the self. You realize that you are a small part of a greater whole and learn to respond appropriately.[23]

It's easy to see why this would be invaluable in mindshifting.

So, stop for a moment.

Put this book down, gently.

Sit back. Close your eyes. Take three deep breaths. Open your eyes slowly, and...

Look up.

What do you see?

A ceiling? The sky? Light fixtures? Whatever it is, take a moment and just gaze at it, no matter how boring it might seem. Take three deep breaths. Now try to find something unique in what's above you. Notice details you might haven't noticed before. Or try to find patterns or connection points. Ask questions.

Then, start to wonder about it. Whatever it is. Just wonder.

Make time to keep finding moments to feel wonder. As you do, you will not only stimulate your curiosity, you'll gain a perspective that's not only more open and acute, but also enlightened. The Greek philosopher Socrates once stated, "Wonder is the beginning of wisdom." People around you will notice. You'll show up differently in each moment and with others. You'll think about problems, challenges, threats, and opportunities with more openness and creativity. And you will inspire people to join you in your mindshift.

Make time to keep finding moments to feel wonder.

Chapter 7

Receive

What a journey
we've been on.
Just look at
how far we've
already come.

Together

...we've learned that the door is opening to a novel economy, and it's an era that needs new leadership.

...learned that even though executives might think they do, they don't always have all the answers.

...explored the great empathy divide between executives and employees and also executives and customers.

...recognized that we can drive change and progress and not have to wait for someone else to do it for us.

...learned that as we start the mindshift journey, we must be aware that our life and work experiences can work against us.

...learned to cultivate self-awareness and to watch out for dangerous biases.

...challenged ourselves to recognize the limitations and vicious cycle of fixed mindsets and to embrace the possibilities of a growth mindset and its virtuous cycle.

...opened our minds to a reset, to set ourselves free from an expert's constraints, and to see the world as beginners.

...reignited our senses of curiosity and wonder to spark creative thinking and ideation.

...learned that by experiencing awe, we can chart a course toward leadership through self-actualization and eventually becoming that leader through self-transcendence, the true Mecca of mindshifting.

You're now ready to go ahead and lead a Mindset Revolution.

6 Stages of
Mindset Shifting

Achieve

Receive

Conceive

Believe

Weave

Perceive

These are the six stages of mindset shifting, which form a virtuous cycle of transformation

1. **Receive:** This is where our open mind gives way to receive signals that we weren't receiving before, namely, emergent trends and potential harbingers of disruption. With a receiver's mind, you become open to new and relevant signals, in whatever form they may arrive. You're more apt to listen, observe, process. You allow yourself to unleash imagination and creativity.

2. **Perceive:** Analyze signals, trends, and harbingers to understand their meaning and potential impact. Assess threats and opportunities. Organize by themes. Capture the story outline and narrative for important trends.

3. **Weave:** Measure the true potential of each trend to specifically validate and prioritize each according to threat/opportunity, market trajectory, and business impact.

4. **Conceive:** The more impactful trends will be weaved into stories that compel decision-makers and stakeholders to move the needle. It's through the power of your storytelling that you gain true influence.

5. **Believe:** In order to catalyze change, your story must be believable. It's with believability that you move people to care; to open their hearts and minds and join in your mindshift.

6. **Achieve:** Once a case is made or a sense of urgency is ignited, planning and strategy become the mechanism to take action. You and those you've inspired lead the change you've envisioned in an infectious spirit of proactive transformation.

To make this mindshift journey, you will engage a set of tools, which I will introduce, to identify the transformation you want to lead and then bring others along.

Here is our mindshift lexicon:

Trendsight: The lens through which you observe the present and look to the horizon.

Trendsighting: The act of observing, assembling, and understanding potentially impactful trends and events, now and in the future.

Trendscape canvas: The process of assessing, categorizing, prioritizing, and describing trends and events and the potential impact on your world now and in the future.

Trendfluence: The acts of relating to and engaging others to connect, inspire, and motivate them to see the potential for different actions to open and shift mindsets toward growth.

Trendspark: Catalyzing action to respond accordingly, to change course in daily routines and, ultimately, new trajectories.

Let's get started here, with receiving.

This begins with recognizing what you know, what you know you don't know, and what you don't know you don't know.

"What you know" equals your "one book."

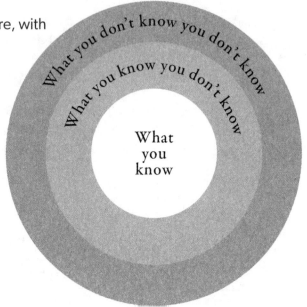

"What you know you don't know" symbolizes self-awareness and sets the stage for unlearning and learning.

"What you don't know" you don't know can signify either opportunity or ignorance.

Embracing "what you don't know you don't know" is essential to discovering opportunities. It reminds you to open your mind, to be a beginner, and to scan the horizon of emerging trends with a sense of wonder.

This is the essence of a *receiver's state of mind*, one that is not just empty but ready to receive and excited about steering toward what lies ahead. With a receiver's mind, we become open to new and relevant signals, in whatever form they may arrive. We're more apt to listen, observe, process, and then consider the best way to respond and move forward. We allow ourselves to unleash imagination and creativity and to respond with an open heart and mind.

As you start scanning for signals, you have to slow down.

Slow Down

I remember recently racing to get the family ready to see my parents and sister's family for a dinner in Santa Monica, California. My dad loves watches. So, I grabbed my favorite watch, one I knew he might appreciate, and went to strap it on while walking over to the closet. The clasp didn't catch, and the watch dropped face down onto stone tiles. I held my breath as I picked it up to examine any potential damage, and sure enough, I cracked the crystal.

I sighed out loud.

My wife asked what happened and after I explained, she said, "That's a sign that you're too hurried, running around, and not taking your time to focus." My mind wasn't open to receiving. She was right.

We have to slow down.

Those words would come to haunt me again just a year later, when I cut my hand wide open trying to open a bottle of wine. I'll save you the gory details, but in hindsight, I distinctly remember my mind not being in that moment. Something in the back of my mind told me not to open the bottle. There were other things to do, and a glass of wine could wait.

I wasn't in the moment. An accident happened. I needed surgery. Afterward, I still didn't slow down. I re-injured my hand and had to go back for a second surgery. Let me tell you something. I slowed down. I became more mindful. And I practice it every day.

We can't receive new signals and can't see the need to improve or detour or change if we're moving too fast.

Reflecting, I wondered how many times in other scenarios my mind had not been in the moment. How many times did I receive signals and dismiss them out of busyness? How many times did I dismiss signals? Or how many times did I receive a signal, initially recognize it, and then dismiss it because I felt too busy to think about it?

So slow down. Pay attention. Listen. Open your heart and mind. Visualize life slowing down. Allow yourself time to receive. Signals do not arrive in the form of a golden ticket in our favorite chocolate bar. Clouds do not part in the sky to reveal a sign. Most of the time, we encounter important signals in everyday moments of life.

In 2014, Radboud University Nijmegen wrote a paper explaining that the brain works like a radio receiver.[1] Here, we want to tune it to focus on emerging trends.

Receiving signals is the process of trendsighting. It's the practice of collecting information to spot patterns and recognize any potential promise in the emergent trends we're tracking. It's understanding and balancing the inherent possibilities and impact and the risk versus reward tied to each trend we study. The art is to see the prospective future of each trend and its market impact beyond the trend itself. How might it play out over time?

Emergent trends across the trendscape are comprised of patterns that indicate gradual changes in condition, output, or process. Over time, these changes become more prominent in their measures, ultimately affecting behaviors.[2] They become disruptive when they restructure, reshape, or transform how we work and/or live.

Early on, as we're learning not just how to track trends but also how to identify them, letting go of the burden of trying to predict the future.[3] That's not what we're trying to do here. We are exploring the trends that might impact our ecosystem. It's a process of getting smart about the promise or potential of emerging trends. It's also spending time thinking about how those trends could unfold and what those changes might look like.

Trendsighting helps us to understand the following[4]:

- The societal trends we should consider in our work, planning, and, strategy
- How these trends can disrupt our vision
- How these trends inspire new ideas
- How these trends can unlock competitive potential and advantages
- How longer-term trends affect our business strategy and product roadmap

How do we know which trends to pay attention to and which are merely fads, and how do we discern between trends that carry impact that can evolve into micro, macro, and megatrends over time? Don't worry. We don't need to figure it all out right now. We'll perfect your process and sharpen your senses as you go.

You can start by considering the following:

- Trends affecting our business that are overlooked or underrated
- Trends affecting how we work
- Trends shifting customer and employee behaviors, expectations, and preferences
- Skills needed to work effectively as technologies and needs evolve, i.e., genAI, AR/VR, robotics, 3D immersive web, et al.
- Soft or human skills that must be developed, such as empathy, creativity, listening, relationship-building/networking, adaptability, resilience, and collaboration
- Younger generations and how they reshape the future of our markets

As you contemplate these trends, ask yourself these questions:

- What do you want or need to learn?
- Who are the experts you can learn from?
- What are the sources of information and events that might introduce you to trends?

As you go through this process, take time to do the following:

Wonder

Capture all the questions you have. What are all the things that inspire you in your life or work? What confuses you? What keeps you up at night? What's most interesting to you?

A great way to do this is to create a wonder wall, which is a powerful exercise in creative expression and exploration. You write down your questions, maybe on scraps of paper or post-it notes, and pin or tape them to a board or wall. Or you can create your wonder wall digitally. A wonder wall is the visual reflection of the things that stoke your curiosity and the things that you can't stop thinking about, that are burning inside of you. In the song "Wonderwall" by Oasis, wonderwall refers to the person you are completely infatuated with. Here it is the possibilities for the future that excite you.

Creating a wonder wall activates your powers of curiosity. It helps you connect the dots between the future you envision and where you are today. The process ignites your childlike sense of wonder and helps you consider the questions with a beginner's mind and a positive sense of the possibilities. Here is a set of questions I've found of great help:

Discover

Write a few sentences to articulate your why...your purpose. Why do these areas of interest compel you? What is it you're so passionate about and why? What is it about these perspectives that burns so brightly inside of you? Later, when things get more formalized, harder, and real, you'll look back to this statement to *remember why you started.*

Get input

Find your influencers and experts by topic and idea. Focus on those whose thinking and style connect with your aspirations, not biases or predispositions, and those who push your thinking. Tune everything else out that doesn't help, stimulate, or provoke your growth.

Tip: Let influencers and experts know how you've helped them. They love to hear it, and they'll remember you.

Engage

Join communities with your peers who are engaging with one another to ask and answer similar questions or those who spark dialogue important to your quest to learn and unlearn and grow.

Participate

Attend industry events that push your thinking and actions forward. Challenge yourself to get out of your comfort zone. For example, it's easy to attend local events, but the stimulation may not be of the caliber necessary to challenge and provoke your thinking. When I want to open my mind, learn, or challenge myself, I look at identifying the right events, even if I have to travel. I say yes to events or engagements that push me out of my comfort zone, and I pay attention to what others are saying, even if I disagree with them, to understand a fuller array of dynamics at play. For example, I fly to Cerebral Valley aka San Francisco to participate in AI events hosted by industry leaders to learn and network.

Study

Absorb up-to-date industry research at macro and micro levels. Sometimes your organization may already have access to these reports. Oftentimes, the press covers higher-profile reports so that you can at least get a summary of trends. In other cases, libraries may have access to key reports. For example, the British Library's Business & IP Centre houses more than £5m worth of online market reports from top publishers such as Mintel, Frost & Sullivan, Euromonitor, and many more, as well as up-to-date sector and company data for more than 144 million UK and global companies.[5]

Listen

Don't listen to hear or just repeat what you heard. Listen to empathize. Listen to unlearn and learn. Listen to challenge your own conventions. Listen to see what others are missing. Talk to colleagues, customers, and partners to get their thoughts and feelings on important subjects. And don't just talk to those who align with your thinking or who validate your presumptions or beliefs. Find those who are also cynical and detractors, those who see things differently, to open your mind further and inspire how you solve problems and create opportunities.

Compare

Look at competitors, including what they're saying, what they're doing, and, more so, what they're not saying or doing. Study leaders and leading companies in other industries and observe their activities. Reverse-engineer what they are doing well to re-create those activities in your realm.

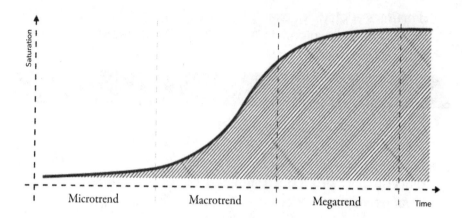

Understanding Four Basic Trends to Frame Our Work in Receiving and Perceiving

Agreat way to categorize trends is by potential time frames. Let's break them down, organized by impact and timespans.[6]

If we were to visualize trends organized by market impact in the y-axis and time in the x-axis, fads, microtrends, macrotrends, and megatrends grow in pervasiveness/saturation over time. But not every trend spans the life cycle from fad to megatrend. Some fizzle out along the way.

Fad: A *fad* is a trend that's suddenly everywhere, quickly gaining in popularity and then fading away almost as quickly. For parents out there, we can look at the most popular toys each Christmas to see examples of fads that come and go.

Just because some people think it's a fad doesn't mean it's not important in our work. We have to keep up a guard against the nahs, huhs, no ways, whatevers, and hems and haws. Sometimes that person can be us.

Fad Product	Time of Popularity
Lava lamps	1970s with a 1990s resurgence
Hacky sacks	Biggest in the 1980s with a 1990s resurgence
Jelly shoes	1980s
Cabbage Patch dolls	1980s
Rubik's cubes	1980s with several subsequent resurgences
Furbys	1990s
Beanie Babies	1990s
Push Pops & Ring Pops	1990s and early 2000s
Polly Pocket	1990s and early 2000s
Razor scooters	2000s
Bratz dolls	2001
Hoverboards	2014
Fidget spinners	2017
Fidget Bubbles Pop Its	2022

I remember thinking pickleball was going to be a fad. So many customers I was studying as part of a particular industry shared a notable overlap in a Venn diagram with pickleball. I thought that the overlap between the emerging sport and customer interest in products and services related to romantic relationships was due to COVID-born boon for the sport. People wanted to get outside and be active. Single people were looking for others to spend time with, and pickleball seemingly offered a safe and fun activity and outdoor venue to do so. The sport served as a safe and exciting way to meet others with similar interests.

Lo and behold, this was just one of the many drivers that made pickleball a would-be fad that turned into a microtrend that's grown into a macrotrend. What's interesting is that this macrotrend is now affecting other sports, causing a potential riff between clubs that are dedicated to tennis as they convert tennis courts into pickleball courts.

I didn't know this, but pickleball got its start in 1965 and has steadily built a following over the years.[7] In fact, it's become the fastest growing sport in the United States.[8] Total pickleball participation grew 85.7% in 2022 and grew 41% over a three-year average. At the casual level (playing one to seven times a year), participants grew 92.5% year over year, up 47.6% over a three-year average.[9]

It's a fad that became a micro trend that became a macro trend. What's interesting is that macro trends are going back down the hierarchy and creating micro trends in tennis club transformation.

According to the Association of Pickleball Professionals,[10] more than 23.6 million people played tennis in the United States in 2022. While you might think that tennis is the more popular sport among the masses, the total number of tennis players equates to 12.9 million, fewer than the number of people who played pickleball, which is estimated at 36.5 million in the same time frame. Now many athletic clubs and parks are converting tennis courts into pickleball courts, which, as you can imagine, puts decision-makers in a pickle.[11]

The point is that trends can lead to change, and for those who are paying attention, the change that's needed to survive and thrive rarely comes as a surprise. When it comes to my work, understanding how social connections and romance and love unfold in the Venn diagram that includes pickleball, I'll put it this way, I'll dink to that. I've since learned that when it comes to couples play, love always happens in the kitchen (it's an inside joke—pun intended).

Microtrends: *Microtrends* are slower in development than fads but represent trends that will most likely hit with a much wider impact and scale than a fad. Experts suggest a span of three to five years.[12] In 2020 micro trends such as working from home and e-commerce became the new norm almost overnight. But these trends were long in the making with remote work or "telecommuting" dating back to the 1970s and 1980s and e-commerce taking off in the 1990s. In the days since COVID-19, working from home and e-commerce have dipped in their pervasiveness and persistence.

In 2023, executives started making headlines as they attempted to bring employees back to the office. While peaking in 2020 to 14.9% from 10.3% in 2019, higher than anticipated before the pandemic, e-commerce fell to 12.2% in 2021.[13] This doesn't mean these movements are fading away; it just means that for now, they are micro trends that could one day become micro trends again or evolve into macro trends.

In all honesty, the difference between a fad and a microtrend, at least early on, is measured in time and impact. But these are difficult to distinguish early on, and even the best of us has a hard time discerning between them. We may in fact intentionally dedicate time and resources to understand trends that end up fizzling out like shooting stars. It's a fine line that separates trends from fads, and that's OK. We're not wasting our time. We're practicing. And more so, fads have a way of influencing the next big thing. So, we're also honing our skills of receiving and perceiving. It's better to be on the side of awareness than ignorance. But if lessons in my studies have taught me one thing, it's that even fads have a way of reappearing as trends later.

For example, in 2022, NFTs, Web3, and the Metaverse were all the rage, taking over the headlines of business and technology media, including fashion and lifestyle press. By 2023, each in their own way had dropped below at least mainstream radar, with some wondering if these technologies equated to fads that fizzled out as quickly as they hit the stage.

Macrotrends: Macrotrends manifest in zeitgeists. They are slow in taking shape but potent in bringing about change. They gain broader market prevalence and persistence, spurring a large-scale, sustained shift in behavior that can last for five to ten years or more.[14] Macrotrends affect larger populations, creating or shifting entire market segments. They also affect the environment or ecosystem in which you operate, even if the business isn't directly related to the trend's core, focus, or subject area.[15]

Think about when the iPhone was first introduced in 2007 and went on to become the most popular phone that year.[16] The previous year, 2006, the Motorola RAZR, an ultra-thin clamshell "fashion phone" was among the most popular devices.[17] The iPhone would become a macrotrend of its own, disrupting the entire phone market and also spurring a macrotrend of smartphones powered by Google Android, with the first, the HTC Dream, debuting in 2008.[18]

Another example of a macrotrend is social media, although early on each social network represented a potential fad, which evolved into microtrends that, when combined, snowballed into a world-changing macrotrend. Six Degrees is widely considered as the first social networking site, which launched in 1997.[19] Early social networks Friendster and MySpace debuted in 2003.[20] Facebook opened the doors to its social network to the public in 2006.[21] Twitter took flight after presenting at the South by Southwest music and technology conference in 2007.[22] Instagram launched in 2010.[23] Snapchat followed in 2011.[24]

Eventually social media, network by network, evolved into a macrotrend that would democratize media and change how the world connects and communicates. It would also go on to spark micro- and macrotrends of their own across industries.

- Disinformation
- Mental health effects
- Polarization of networks
- Influencers as celebrities
- Social commerce
- Social media users as a new genre of creators

We could explore an entire book's worth (actually more like volumes of books) of examples of fads, microtrends, and macrotrends. One last to mention is the shift from work from home as a microtrend to hybrid work as a macrotrend. Companies are expected to be more flexible in where they ask employees to work. It will be a balance between the office and remote. Hybrid work is here to stay. And companies will reimagine what commercial workspace looks like to be more enticing, intuitive, and alluring to employees. Sixty-six percent of leaders state that their company thinks about redesigning office spaces for hybrid work.[25]

Megatrends: *Megatrends* are products of zeitgeists. They "identify and describe extremely complex change dynamics and are a model for the transformation of the world," lasting a minimum of several decades.[26] They move slowly, but with enormous strength.

Megatrends serve as windows into the future.[27] The Copenhagen Institute for Future Studies[28] defines Megatrends as the "the probable future—or express what we know with great confidence about the future. Megatrends are certainties."

BlackRock describes megatrends as "powerful, transformative forces that could change the global economy, business, and society."

It's the trend and how the trend reshapes the world that makes it a megatrend. For example, past megatrends include electricity, automobiles, the Internet, mobile devices, and the Internet of Things. While each trend was transformative, they created waves of new capabilities, products, ecosystems, and behaviors that, in many cases, are still evolving.[29]

Another example includes EVs. Tesla sparked a modern-day race toward the shift from internal combustion engine (ICE) vehicles to electric vehicles (EVs). EVs becoming the dominant form of transportation is in itself a megatrend. Consider that many are already capable of self-driving. At some point, owning a car in city centers will become a service. Garages, parking lots, and gas stations will make space for reimagined development to support self-driving vehicles as an on-demand, shared, or subscription service. In-car experiences will make vehicle interiors resemble a lounge or office instead of a traditional cockpit.

Think about something as seemingly random as organ transplants. With self-driving vehicles theoretically much safer than those driven by humans, there's a great likelihood that organ transplants will decline.[30] We were given a preview of what could happen with COVID-19 lockdowns.[31] This scenario is something experts have been thinking about for more than a decade. Investments in solutions such as 3D printing and bioengineering are now being cultivated to potentially generate organs ahead of the shortage.[32]

With the launch of ChatGPT in 2022, the potential of artificial intelligence (AI) was popularized, and a new emerging megatrend was born. AI will impact every sector, every product and service, how we work, and nearly every other megatrend.[33]

Other megatrends the world's experts are tracking include climate change, resource scarcity, and shifting economic power as China becomes a new superpower and India threatens to rival the United States.[34]

Understanding how to categorize these trends helps us see the novelty, potentiality, or gravitas in what we're tracking. It helps us then perceive how we prioritize and organize trends and, then, what we do about them. A great tool for thinking about where a trend might be on the timeline is the Hype Cycle, developed by Gartner.

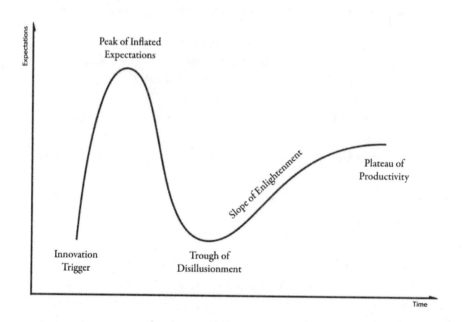

I'm a big fan because all emerging trends that gain any type of traction will usually earn a spot on its list of technologies to watch.[35] What makes the Hype Cycle so interesting is its name. Hype is part of the life cycle for most trends. Even those that emerge out of stealth or out of nowhere will have to find a place in this world to survive and thrive as technologies mature. Some might pan out as fads. Others will become the drivers of new applications and behavior changes. Either way, according to Gartner, most tend to follow a path from innovation to a "peak of inflated expectations," aka "hype," toward a Ctrl+Alt+Del moment. From there, trends either fade into obscurity or find a new life rooted in specific, more commercially viable applications.

Gartner's Hype Cycle tracks trends for those of us paying attention. It helps us understand the trajectory of trends, where they are at a specific point in time, and how long it may take each trend to find their potential sweet spot (mass market adoption), if at all. It's organized by "expectations" in the y-axis and "time" in the x-axis. The potential of each trend and its life span are defined by their relevance to solving real-world problems or exploiting new opportunities. The Hype Cycle curve exists within this construct, organized in the following stages (as defined by Gartner):[36]

Innovation trigger: A potential technological breakthrough kicks things off. Early proof-of-concept stories and media interest trigger significant publicity. Often no usable products exist, and commercial viability is unproven.

Peak of inflated expectations: Early publicity produces several success stories—often accompanied by scores of failures. Some companies act; many do not.

Trough of disillusionment: Interest wanes as experiments and implementations fail to deliver. Producers of the technology shake out or fail. Investments continue only if the surviving providers improve their products to the satisfaction of early adopters.

Slope of enlightenment: More instances of how the technology can benefit the enterprise start to crystallize and become more widely understood. Second- and third-generation products appear from technology providers. More enterprises fund pilots; conservative companies remain cautious.

Plateau of productivity: Mainstream adoption starts to take off. Criteria for assessing provider viability are more clearly defined. The technology's broad market applicability and relevance are clearly paying off.

Whether we're tracking technology or market or cultural trends, we develop a model that helps us identify what matters, why, and where these trends are in their life cycle. While not an exact science, gaining an understanding about trends will help us nurture our curiosity, our ability to mitigate risk, and our capacity to identify opportunities to thwart disruption and create new value.

I take a human-centered perspective when I look for and examine trends. This perspective places people at the center of decision-making, ideation, and development. I learned a lot by studying the work of IDEO, a global design company I've followed for years. I'm a big fan of David Kelley, founder, and Tom Kelley, partner. Their book, *Creative Confidence*, gave me the confidence to reignite creativity in my work. IDEO has contributed toward the evolution of design thinking,[37] a process that integrates the needs of people, the possibilities of technology, and the requirements for business success.[38] It's IDEO's approach to design thinking that can help us think about trends and how we rationalize and qualify them in our discovery process.

Design thinking helps achieve that balance. It lets people find the sweet spot of feasibility, viability, and desirability while considering the real needs and desires of people. Thinking like a designer can transform the way organizations develop products, services, processes, and strategy. This approach brings together what is desirable from a human point of view with what is technologically feasible and economically viable. It also allows people who aren't trained as designers to use creative tools to address a vast range of challenges.

Some questions I like to think through as I discover and value trends include the following:

- Does this trend represent the ability to affect people who matter to me? Do people get it? Is it intuitive/easily understood? Does it scale?
- Does it solve an unaddressed problem or solve an existing problem in an ingenious way?
- Does it create new value or provide newfound utility?
- Does this trend represent the capacity to change behaviors?

All of this trendsighting will help us understand where to invest more time in learning and scenario planning and potentially where to experiment and develop proofs of concepts.

Now it's time to perceive and to dig into what all of this information you've gathered about trends may have to tell you about the change you should lead.

Chapter 8

Perceive

In this next phase, we organize our inputs so we can begin evaluating which trends are important, what's worth tracking, and what's not useful now.

Our power to perceive is the ability to:

see a situation, event, or trend;

analyze, study, and understand it;

assess opportunities and solutions, risks, and threats; and

define the next necessary steps.

Those are the goals of this step. This is where you will develop your trendscape canvas. It's the foundation for centralizing, organizing, and, eventually, telling your story about the future that compels people to mindshift.

In my work, I track trends that impact business-to-business (B2B) and business-to-consumer (B2C) markets across multiple industries. And they're always evolving. My goal is to help executives understand these trends and, even more, to create a sense of urgency about responding to them.

Recognizing trends and connecting the dots among them aren't skills we master overnight. It takes technique and practice. The good news is that we get better as we go. There is no one way to do this, but I've found the following is a core set of best practices:

1. **Record:** Capture what you're receiving onto lists or models of your choosing. Try to keep the list manageable and focused on what's important to your organization (and you), guided by your vision and purpose.

2. **Categorize:** Identify and organize topics and trends by patterns. Sort parts by themes. Once your themes are defined and described, organize by patterns that impact the business. Create a "parking lot" where you place trends that appear important but don't yet line up with the themes that stand out now. You don't want to lose track of them.

3. **Substantiate:** Collect data and references that substantiate each trend.

4. **Evaluate:** Add dimensionality to your catalog by qualifying trends for further study. One way to do so is to create a 2x2 organized by Short- and Long-Term on the x-axis and Market Impact and Business Impact on the y-axis. Place each trend accordingly on the matrix. Those that end up in the upper-right quadrant should make the list of trends worthy of attention. The others should be placed in the parking lot.

5. **Prioritize:** Rank trends or events by urgency, importance, and those worthy of further study. Measures can include current state/urgency, business impact, opportunity cost, market alignment, and risk. I use a spider graph model to evaluate each trend. Separate them into short- and long-term opportunities and those to keep in a parking lot.

Tip: This methodology can also apply to organizing and enhancing your personal life and career.

I created this basic template that you can use and build upon for your trendscape canvas. Each section is populated with sample trends I was tracking at the time of writing this section. You should feel free to use it, but also to develop your own format, in whatever way you prefer. I will explain how to fill in each part.

Record

In the receive stage, we've spent a great deal of time learning about all the trends emerging and circling our business and industry. To say it's overwhelming and exciting and scary only partially captures the emotions I'm sure you've felt in the process.

Recording is the process of cataloging and putting into order all the trends we've been learning about and capturing. We won't track everything. The following activities will help us focus, qualify, merge, and even set aside some of the vast array of trends.

Recording is the path toward focusing the signals in our receiver's state to capture what matters now, next year, a few or several years from now, and even a decade away.

Record

PATTERN: [Name Theme]

[Organize trends into themes. Explain what's happening using the language of laypeople.] Emergent apps and products are reshaping customer attention, behaviors, expectations, and preferences. Mobile-first and new UI/UX-driven behaviors are making customers move faster, becoming impatient digital experiences that don't perform against expectations.

PATTERN: New Consumerism

Accidental Narcissists: A more connected, informed, fast-paced, distracted consumer is emerging. They expect engagement to be hyper- personalized, intuitive, efficient, and anticipatory of their needs and desired outcomes.

Generation Novel: How the pandemic opened people's hearts and minds, changing their values and what they value and creating a cross-generational consumer who shops and works differently than groups before them and greater than any one generational demographic.

Digital Introverts: Customers are learning to become self-sufficient in the experiences and outcomes they seek. When possible, they would like to be engaged personally, but also digitally, to optimize their time. Humans play a role when they can add value or a VIP touch.

PATTERN: Innovation Targeting New Consumers

Company A saw a gap in the market and introduced X to disrupt the market and attract customers seeking Y experiences/products/outcomes...

Company B reimagined customer service and/or marketing or commerce or loyalty by mimicking Company A and doing 1, 2, 3...

Technology C radically transformed how customers interact online making our touch points and customer journey potentially obsolete.

PATTERN: Disrupted Companies That Failed

Company A failed because they didn't do 1, 2, 3.

Company B overcame a challenge by doing 1, 2, 3.

Company C transformed by doing 1, 2, 3.

Company D was created to deliver 1, 2, 3 because incumbents missed their window.

To get us started, I wanted to share some high-level trends I was tracking as part of a series of projects for companies at the time of writing this book. These are the tools I use in my work at ServiceNow as head of global innovation to track emerging technologies and their potential effects on B2B and consumer behaviors.

Here are some questions to consider:

- Of all the trends and events that seem interesting, which would you categorize as fads versus micro events that could potentially add up to bigger "macro" impacts? Are there any trends that represent emergent macro trends that may already be cresting as a wave rolling toward crashing on the shore of your business?

- How can these trends help you, your team, and your organization thrive and grow as aligned with the goals and objectives of the business? Why are they important to not miss?

- What are the business problems that these emergent trends solve?

- What new problems do these trends potentially create for you and the company? What are the possible opportunity costs of not exploring these trends?

- What are the upsides or new business opportunities that these trends unlock for the company? How can they become a competitive or first-mover advantage?

- What are clear ways that you can connect the dots back to your purpose, your team's, and other stakeholders and decision-makers?

When I was writing this chapter, I reviewed a few of my trendscape canvases that captured some of the key trends I was tracking. It reminded me that many technologies were accelerated when the world was thrust into a digital-first society between 2020–2023. There was a permanent shift, radically shortening the waves of industry-transforming innovation. AI, augmented/virtual reality, robotics, spatial computing, hybrid experiences, decentralized identity, Web3, digital twins, digital humans…the list goes on.

After leaving Altimeter Group, the analyst firm I helped build, I no longer had access to an infrastructure for dedicated research. Partner firms such as Gartner, Forrester, and IDC became instrumental in augmenting my work.

The Gartner "Emerging Technologies and Trends Impact Radar"[1] visually explores trends organized by patterns, and themes, substantiated by Gartner analysts who study emergent trends and their impact on business. In this particular 2023 example, there were four patterns comprised of technology themes.

I summarize them this way:

- The smart world expands with the fusion of physical-digital experiences.
- Productivity accelerates with AI advances.
- Transparency/privacy get scrutiny amid exponential growth in data collection.
- New critical tech enablers create new business and monetization opportunities.

Each trend is also based on its potential opportunity and threat to organizations and organized on a horizonal plane that spans a time frame (zero to one year, one to three years, three to six years, and six to eight years). Each horizon is denoted by a certain color to visually represent where each trend resides on the timeline. Those trends that are not critical to each pattern were moved to my parking lot.

The Gartner radar served as a strategic ally in understanding trends' potential impacts on businesses (and market behaviors). I wanted to share some of the signals the discovery work in my receiver's state identified as potential trends. Through a partial snapshot in time, they're representative of the types of trends that would populate your trendscape canvas. Use them as an illustration for the signals and trends you will identify and track in your own work.

- Micro trends affecting or influencing how customers experience companies and their products and services
    - Mobile-first and new UI/UX-driven behaviors (we will examine this trend throughout the chapter)
    - Apps and products that reshape customer attention, behaviors, expectations, and preferences

The distinction here is that mobile devices, such as iPhone and Androids, and popular apps are conditioning customers to act and think differently. This evolution is outpacing the customer experience most companies provide their customers. It sets the stage for micro- and then macro-disruption as more and more customers are likely to find alternatives that better match their behaviors, lifestyle, and standards for engagement.

- Cultural, societal, and emotional trends that affect consumer decision-making, affinity, and loyalty
- Best-in-class customer experience trends inspired by trends or disrupting markets
- Leadership and stakeholder dynamics to connect the dots between trends, business goals and opportunities, executive priorities and strategies, and investments in operational, business model, and digital transformation
- Best-in-class examples of transformation, innovation, and new leadership

Categorize (Themes and Patterns)

It's way too easy for everything to become interesting and then, very quickly, overwhelming. Think of your trends as playing cards. Depending on the game we may play, after the cards are dealt, we pick up the cards and fan them out. This helps us recognize themes and how they connect, to group them by suit, color, or sequence. You'll start to see broader patterns that come together much in the same way winning hands are organized in a card game.

This categorization is important for several reasons that go beyond the process of placing trends into groups. It also helps us hone our ability to spot trends and identify how they fit with one another. It helps us understand the importance of the bigger trends that each represent as a whole. This helps demonstrate significance and perhaps even urgency.

Our curiosity will naturally shape internal mechanisms or filters we use to align the trends we observe with our work and our purpose. The art of observation, organization, and understanding becomes perfected by the narrative we tell ourselves as to why each trend is important now and why they're likely to be even more important in the future.

Record: Organize trends/signals as patterns.

- What do these patterns represent as opportunities or threats or as areas of further study?
- Why might they be important to your organization? What does each mean?
- What questions do they raise?
- Which of these trends overlap and/or gain strength if they're combined?

Categorize
THEME 1: [NAME] CX Modernization
[Description] Trends affecting or influencing how customers experience companies and their products and services
THEME 2: Consumer Decision-Making/Relationships
Cultural, societal, and emotional trends that affect consumer decision-making, affinity, and loyalty
THEME 3: CX Innovation + Operational Transformation
Best-in-class customer experience trends advancing as a result of disruptive trends and/or innovative companies changing the game
THEME 4: Corporate Innovation + Disruption
Leadership and stakeholder dynamics to connect the dots between trends, business goals and opportunities, executive priorities and strategies, and investments in operational, business model, and digital transformation
Best-in-class examples of transformation, innovation, and new leadership

Categorize: Organize patterns as strategic themes.

- How do patterns add up to meaningful issues, questions, concerns, or ideas?
- How could each represent a threat or opportunity?
- How would patterns get broken into potential strategies for study or action?

Writing these reflections out will help you sharpen your ability to capture the spirit and promise of each trend to get to the source of its meaning and potentiality. Write with others in mind. If someone were to read it, would they get it? Would they react with awe or a sense of urgency, or would their eyes glaze over because they don't get it?

I think about this process as the beginning of crafting the story you will tell to bring others along with your mindshift. Think about the language you can use that will be most activating of people's imaginations and most powerful in inspiring them to act.

As you go through this exercise, there will be trends that naturally connect to others. There may also be one overarching trend that the others will fall under. A good way to organize them is to use the device of writing headers and subheaders. We organized trends we were writing about this way when I was with Altimeter Group, with heads numbered H1, H2, and H3, etc., if necessary.

H1 is reserved for the top of the page. It acts as a headline for the entire structure.[1] This is the overarching trend.

As an example, "The Rise of EVs and the Decline of ICE" could be labeled as the H1 theme. H2s under it could include the following:

- Traditional manufacturers go all in on EVs, marking the beginning of the end for ICE manufacturing.
- Self-driving vehicles have become more commonplace, changing the entire ecosystem for human-driven cars.

H3s here might include the following:

- Investments in alternative organ harvesting spike due to the anticipated drop in fatal accidents that lead to organ donations.
- New insurance products are introduced that cover circumstances and scenarios and technologies powering self-driving cars and entertainment for passengers.

With practice it starts to become clearer which trends align with key themes you identify and what level they are, as well as which you can move to the parking lot. Check on these trends quarterly (or in intervals that make sense for your work) to see if they deserve to move up on your list of trends to track.

Parking Lot
AI-powered, intelligent digital humans supporting the contact center
Quantum computing providing advanced capabilities to scenario plan possible alternative futures
Digital twins for manufacturing digital twins for CX
Metaverse: development for branded 3D, immersive experience that's compatible with universal metaverse standards
Self-driving enterprise powered by AI decision-making in supply chain, pricing and promotion, logistics, sustainability/waste management

Now, take a step back. Look at everything to consider how your themes may help you see bigger patterns.

Ultimately, you will draw on these descriptions for the documents you will share with your audience, whether slides or a report, or both. So when I write these descriptions, I do so with specific people in mind, as if I'm speaking with them, whether it's for someone in finance, human resources, marketing, sales, or the leadership team. I consider how to account for their biases, and I use their language, which helps to encourage their curiosity and to spark questions and dialogue. I also write using simple terms.

Substantiate

Pretend you're an attorney and each trend is your client. To make the case, you have to assemble compelling evidence to convince the judge or jury of its importance. You have to explain why it's worth their time to learn more.

As you build out your trend canvas, add a Substantiate column, where you will assemble high-level evidence with links to supporting materials. Assemble data points and statistics, sound bites, supporting stories, and case studies that help appreciate the gravity of each trend and learn about it more. This is meant to provide the evidence you need at a glance.

Substantiate
THEME 1 SUPPORTING DATA: [NAME] CX Modernization
Data points
Expert quotes
Examples
Reserach reports
Industry articles
THEME 2 SUPPORTING DATA: Consumer Decision-Making/Relationships
Data points
Expert quotes
Examples
Reserach reports
Industry articles
THEME 3 SUPPORTING DATA: CX Innovation + Operational Transformation
Data points
Expert quotes
Examples
Reserach reports
Industry articles
THEME 4 SUPPORTING DATA: Corporate Innovation + Disruption
ROI data points that reflect before and after
Quotes supporting new approaches
Examples
Reserach reports
Industry articles/awards

Check on these trends quarterly (or in intervals that make sense for your work) to see if they deserve to move up on your list of trends to track, to stay on the list, or to fall off.

Evaluate

The goal is to know which trends matter, know how and when a trend might gain momentum, and understand the opportunities and risks each presents. I'll share two models I use to capture and rank trends at a glance and also how I measure, at a high level, their potential impact for prioritization. We can use this tool to help us, at least initially, ascertain whether each trend represents a potential market impact and how that impact may affect our business. As you consider each trend, assess its potential impact in the market and on your business. You may find you need to go back and gather more data or expert opinions to help.

- What are experts predicting?

- What do you believe will happen?

- Why are these trends important to you? To your business? To the ecosystem of your business?

Thinking this through will help you place the trend in the spectrum of high and low impact.

2x2: Behavioral Impact and Business Impact

The first tool is a 2x2 with "Behavioral Impact" on the y-axis and "Business Impact" on the x-axis. You can choose measures that are right for you.

I chose "behavioral" and "business" impacts because innovation and transformation is either the spark or the result of changes in behavior. I study things from a human-centered perspective. If people's behaviors change, markets change. And when markets change, businesses are impacted.

Based on the evidence captured in the substantiate phase, you'll have an idea of where to generally place trends on the 2x2. You will also have data that inspires you to consider the trajectory of each trend.

- Are they trending upward and to the right?

- Is there a hype bubble surrounding it, thus sending it down and to the left?

- Is it too nascent but still potentially promising and worthy of sitting in a parking lot?

Priority Trends

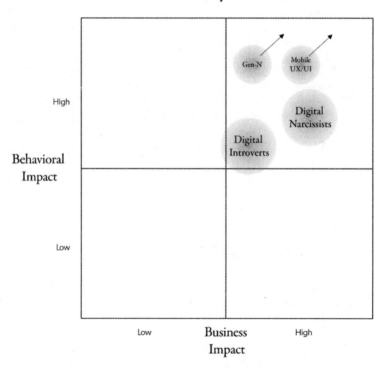

I picked four patterns from the trendscape canvas and then examined the evidence to measure the market impact and business impact of each. Is a trend headed up and to the right? Does it represent a high or low behavioral impact over time? Does it represent a high or low business impact? The lower the trajectory, the more likely it is to represent a fad or microtrend.

As trends veer up and to the right, the more potential they carry to evolve into macro trends and perhaps even megatrends.

To note the difference, use a simple arrow to designate the potential mobility of the trend. You could also use color: short-term = red and long-term = blue.

- Where does the potential for behavioral change rank in the spectrum from high to low? Consider how each trend affects behavior in the short- and long-term.

- How does behavioral change ultimately impact business in the spectrum from high to low or low to high?

- As behavioral change plays out, when does data or expert opinion suggest a potential impact on your business? Is it likely to grow or wane?

Prioritize

The next step in creating your trendscape canvas is to prioritize. That starts with understanding the latency of each trend and prioritizing them based on timing and impact. This will help add the dimension of time for when trends may impact our market and our business and for how long.

Here, we'll explore trends on horizontal levels: Horizon 1, Horizon 2, etc. However, once you get the hang of this process, you can get more detailed by outlining specific timelines and roadmaps. Eventually, we'll use the data and insights we've been tracking to assess each trend more thoroughly to conceive our plan and then to achieve our goals.

Impact and Time

Let's explore two other models that can help us visualize timing and effects as we develop our trendscape canvas, the supporting narrative, and, eventually, our visual storyboard.

I will share two methods I use to further prioritize and visualize trends to help get you started.

Organize by Trend Level and Impact

This first example chart brings together the different classifications of trends, organized by trend level (x) and time/impact (y). This chart denotes the various stages of trends to understand, where possible, when emerging themes/patterns could potentially fall into the spectrum of trend phases: fad, microtrend, macrotrend, and megatrend.

Of all the charts we'll review, this may be the most difficult to practice when we're just getting started. But it's a healthy exercise in understanding how emergent trends evolve and how they may inspire a domino effect of follow-on trends that push trends across the spectrum toward macro- and mega-trends.

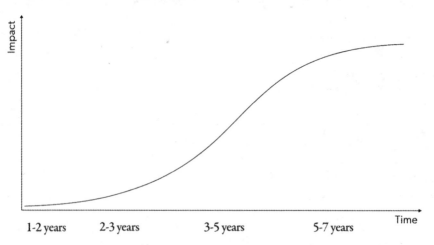

Organize by Time and Impact

The next chart is organized by time (x) and impact (y). Here, time horizons span one to two, two to three, three to five, or five to seven years and help us plot trends against the data we've collected in our earlier work. This chart can help us track trends and their potential impact as they emerge. It can also help track how they evolve and affect markets or behaviors over time. Remember, meaningful trends are rarely static; they're usually in a state of motion. They're either emerging, impacting, or waning. Their position on this or any chart we use will also shift depending on our intervals for revisiting trends (monthly, quarterly, annually).

For example, if we had the foresight to see the inevitable launch of the Apple iPhone in 2007, we could have planned for potential scenarios to accelerate change and innovation in how we work and how we sell.

In hindsight, there are important shifts and milestones that would have served as signals about big shifts in behaviors and market opportunities. Looking back, even as the iPhone launched, many industry leaders balked at its price and ridiculed it for missing a physical keyboard. But within just a few years, data usage on iPhones eclipsed voice usage, and it never looked back. Mobile Internet became dominant. Social media democratized information and influence. Mobile Internet consumption followed TV. AR/VR spawned hybrid applications, bridging physical and online spaces. The next big thing is already taking shape, so what will come, and what will happen next?

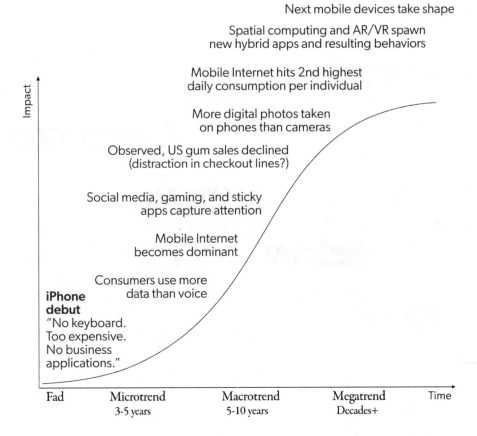

<figure>
Next mobile devices take shape

Spatial computing and AR/VR spawn
new hybrid apps and resulting behaviors

Mobile Internet hits 2nd highest
daily consumption per individual

More digital photos taken
on phones than cameras

Observed, US gum sales declined
(distraction in checkout lines?)

Social media, gaming, and sticky
apps capture attention

Mobile Internet
becomes dominant

Consumers use more
data than voice

iPhone debut
"No keyboard.
Too expensive.
No business
applications."

Impact (y-axis)

Fad | Microtrend 3-5 years | Macrotrend 5-10 years | Megatrend Decades+ | Time
</figure>

Organize by Horizon and Time

Another way to visualize trends is by time (x) and horizon (y). Horizons represent windows to consider timing and duration. And that timing is ours to define. In this example, I mirrored the horizons to the time spans associated with the evolution of trends. Horizons represent windows to consider impact and the relative duration of each. And that impact and duration are ours to define based on research.

The third chart offers flexibility (and approachability) in evaluating and charting trends and when/how they will make an impact. It is designed as a bridge between the first two examples. It helps us practice assembling meaningful trends, understand which of those are likely to impact our business and/or market, understand when they might occur, and figure out how long they may last.

Horizon 1: 18–36 months
Horizon 2: 3–5 years
Horizon 3: 5–7 years
Horizon 4: 7–10+ years

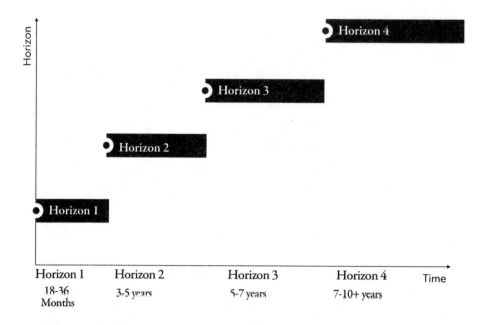

For example, let's take the rise of Generation Novel from the sample trendscape canvas as one instance to examine in terms of horizon and time. Using the evidence gathered to substantiate its place on the canvas, we can go through an exercise of "what it means," in this case, the rise of a connected and conscious consumer who may grow in size, scope, and impact as the trend gathers momentum. The exercise is meant to help scenario plan for potential developments and events to then plan for productive actions and outcomes.

Think of it as a matter of "if this, then that." If this happens, then that would be the impact.

The what.

So what?

Now what?

Horizon 1
Digital narcissists: Self-interested consumers proactively seek intuitive, personalized mobile-first experiences. They start to actively switch brands and crave more meaningful relationships.

Horizon 2
Digital introverts: Fortified by Gen Y, Gen Z and Alpha demand hybrid, immersive, personalized experiences. Values are consequential. AI and AR introduce augmented experiences that facilitate "digital human" + human engagement. Omnichannel is now platform native, creating multiple dynamic journeys.

Horizon 3
Augmented consumerism: Empowered by AI, augmented consumers expect hybrid, immersive, and highly personalized experiences, before they know they need or want them. Engagement shifts to predictive.

Horizon 4
Predictive consumerism: AI and processing power allow for organizations to create digital twins of customer personas to predict behaviors and trends ahead of big decisions + disruptions.

Horizon

Predictive Consumerism

AI and processing power allow for organizations to create digital twins of customer personas to predict behaviors and trends ahead of big decisions + disruptions.

Augmented Consumers

Empowered by AI, augmented consumers expect hybrid, immersive and highly personalized experiences, before they know they need or want them. Engagement shifts to predictive.

Digital Introverts

Fortified by Gen Y, Z, and Alpha, demand for hybrid, immersive, personalized experiences. Values are consequential. AI, AR introduce augmented experiences that facilitate 'digital human' + human engagement. Omni channel is now platform native, creating multiple dynamic journeys.

Gen Z

Digital narcissists. Self-interested consumers proactively seek intuitive, personalized mobile-first experiences. They start to actively switch brands and crave more meaningful relationships.

Horizon 1	Horizon 2	Horizon 3	Horizon 4	Time
18-36 Months	3-5 years	5-7 years	7-10+ years	

These charts are not meant to be perfect. They're intended to help us think through and visualize the trends that we believe are important, when might each trend affect us initially, and what might those impacts look like over time. They're not intended to be exact. You are not nailing exacts. Just know that you have a gift, and it's special. It must be nurtured and put into practice. But even if you're not the next Jeane Dixon, Ray Kurzweil, Aldous Huxley, Peter Schwartz, or the many other visionaries who analyzed trends to envision new possibilities and even new worlds, this is mission-critical work. To be honest, it's also under appreciated at the beginning.

Don't let that dissuade you from becoming the leader this new world so desperately needs.

Chapter 9

Weave

The goal in the next three stages, weave, conceive, and believe, is to develop a story for change that sparks curiosity, conversation, and collaboration, ultimately leading to action.

No matter the evidence we assemble, no matter how convincing the data, it's our story and its ability to connect with and convince our audience that determine the influence and impact we'll have. Stories have more power than any other form of communication to promote understanding and connect people, helping them appreciate the common bonds that bring us together, despite our differences. Stories can build strong communities that band together to write their own version of the future, making that future an incredible story. Professor Scott Galloway observed in his research, "Data may be more truthful, but in the battle between narrative and numbers, most of the time humanity picks narrative."[1]

Storytelling is foundational to mindshifting because it's a powerful means of doing the following:

- Communicating urgency
- Rallying support
- Spotlighting opportunity
- Visualizing a dream
- Uniting stakeholders
- Igniting passion for what's next

Don't worry if you don't think of yourself as a storyteller. We are all storytellers in our own way. In our day-to-day lives, we tell ourselves a story about everything that happens to us to help us make sense of the world. Also, stories don't have to be complex. In fact, some of the best are quite simple.

My friend Michael Margolis, author of *Story 10x: Turn the Impossible Into the Inevitable*, writes, "Story, in its simplest form, is about characters and the things that happen to them." Michael Lewis, author of *Moneyball* and *The Big Short*, defines story simply as "people and situations."[2]

For our purpose, though, to persuade others to mindshift, we want to give our story a sense of urgency; we want to make others see the change we're envisioning and feel our excitement about it. We want to tell the kind of story author Ron Ploof describes. A story, he writes, is a combination of roles (people), events (the things that happen), and the influences (the motivations...why someone takes action).[3]

Many stories intended to spur people to action miss the mark. They're not compelling or thoughtful. They're not inviting or immersive. They don't move people.

By comparison, consider the storytelling of Steve Jobs about Apple's role in our lives. When the iPhone debuted in 2007, people camped out at Apple stores for a chance to be one of the first to own the groundbreaking device. They did so because of Apple's corporate narrative about the brand and what it means in the lives of its customers, its community. I was there in Palo Alto, California. I spent time with people camping out. I captured images of the first customers as they proudly exited the store holding their Apple bags in the air for all to revel in celebration. All these years later, customers still line up for the launch of the latest iPhone.[4] And, just think about a post-iPhone world.

Jobs was a master narrator. He didn't just show us photos of new Apple products. He told us thrilling stories about them. He wove a narrative, telling a story about their enormous value to us. Not every story ranks as a narrative. What is the difference? A narrative is defined as "a way of presenting or understanding a situation or a series of events that reflects and promotes a particular point of view or set of values."[5]

Lots of stories don't do this.

For example, someone downloaded a dating app and was excited to give it a try. They had been lonely for a long time. Too long. While initially anxious and hopeful, they dated so many wrong people that they were losing hope and about to give up. Then, on the last date, they met someone special, their "right person," after a string of "wrongs."

This is a story. But it's not at all compelling. It has the makings to be; there's lots of drama alluded to. But it's not brought to life. We're not really moved to care.

Now consider the extremely short narrative crafted by Guillaume Wiatr, a strategic narrative architect and advisor.[6] He illustrates the power of expressing a point of view in a story with a beautifully simple example. "Someone died" is a story, he writes. But "someone died, and that was very wrong" represents a narrative that "can turn into a revolution."[7]

Weaving a powerful narrative helps to persuade even skeptics, nonbelievers, the biased, and those stuck in their ways and beliefs. Good narratives open minds and hearts.

When we hear the word *weave*, we commonly think of making a cloth or twisting things together to form an object. There's another definition, and it plays a role in how you influence others. To "weave" also means "to *form* something from several different things or to *combine* several different things, in a *complicated* or *skilled* way."[8] And that's what this next step in mindshifting teaches you: how to weave together all that you've been learning about the trends you've identified. This forms the basis of then telling the compelling story about the change you want to advocate.

The trends you're tracking are the foundational elements of your story, and your audience are the characters in it. To make your story compelling, you must do the following:

Contextualize

Contextualizing is about giving meaning to something in ways that are understandable and/or relatable to your audience. Contextualized storytelling shares with the audience not only the "what" but also the why...why it matters to them. Contextualizing frames the story in a way that describes an event, but also the setting, the circumstances, the effects, and what happens next. It connects the dots between a trend and insights, ideas, and takeaways.

It communicates the "what it means" (WIM) for each trend and helps you communicate the what, so what, and now what for your audience of decision-makers and stakeholders.

Contextualized storytelling connects audiences not only to your story but to you as the storyteller.[9] This is because, as neuroscientist Paul J. Zak discovered, stories release oxytocin in the brain, a natural hormone that's also called the "love hormone," helping the audience to feel connected.[10] Oxytocin is also associated with trust building![11] That's clearly very helpful in persuading your audience.

Visualize

Creating compelling visuals helps instill understanding, spark dialogue, nurture alignment, and instigate collaboration and action. Your audience can't always envision the potential impact and opportunity you're describing. You can visualize it for them.

Have you ever shopped for a piece of furniture online but struggled with the process, because you're unsure of what it will look like in your home or office or if it will fit in your space? You aren't alone. Many times, people discover that the furniture they've purchased isn't the right fit only after purchasing it. IKEA aimed to help you solve that problem with its 3D/augmented reality app, IKEA Place.[12] Using your phone or tablet, IKEA Place helps you use augmented reality technology to virtually place furniture in your space.

Visualizing a story is your version of augmented reality, helping your audience see the future you're narrating. Visualization is the art of giving your audience the ability to see and grasp what was previously invisible. French poet, pioneering aviator, and author of *The Little Prince*, Antoine de Saint-Exupéry once wrote, "It is only with the heart that one can see rightly; what is essential is invisible to the eyes." To see rightly, in his view, opens our hearts and minds to help us see things previously hidden.[13]

To get started with crafting your story, you first have to think through the story you want to tell. Then you can work on contextualizing and visualizing it.

Storytelling Begins with Thinking Through What You Want to Convey

Working on your story is a process of thinking through all you've learned so far. Larry McEnerny is a now-retired former director of the University of Chicago's Writing Program. In a class of his I sat in on, he explained that expert writers write to think. They use the writing process to help themselves think, and that's how they do their best thinking.[14] "Ninety-nine percent of experts write and think at the same time," McEnerny explained.

McEnerny also taught that one of the reasons it's so hard for smart people to write well is that they're not engaging in writing for a larger purpose. They don't write to change the way people think about the world. They write to complete a project, to earn a grade, or to be assessed by their teachers or leaders. Or they share their thoughts without going through a mental and soulful exercise of thinking about how to see the world differently.

This is not you. You are writing your story to inspire your audience to change the way they think about the world. But, of course, to do that, you have to change the way you think about the world. Working on crafting your story will make you do this. Going through the exercise is richly rewarding. Allow yourself to take your time with it.

What Is the Why?

When I think of storytelling, I can't help but think of Disney and Pixar. Though they're part of the same organization today, each grew to master the art and science of storytelling in their own special way. If we can glean a fraction of what they can teach us, our storytelling capabilities will take us to new heights.

Pete Docter, film director at Pixar, described the importance of storytelling this way:

> "What you're trying to do, when you tell a story, is to write about an event in your life that made you feel some particular way. And what you're trying to do, when you tell a story, is to get the audience to have that same feeling."[15]

That means you're trying to get the audience to have the same feeling of wonder, awe, inspiration, and urgency about the future you're describing as you do. So, take some time to get in touch with your feelings about how important the change you're advocating is.

Pixar's approach to storytelling encourages storytellers to answer the following four questions before they begin:

- Why must you tell this story?
- What's the belief burning within you that your story feeds off?
- Why will the audience leave better after your story than before they heard it?
- What greater purpose does this serve? What does it teach? What change will it inspire?[16]

You already have some part of the answer to all of these questions:

- You must tell this story first and foremost, because you care. You care about the future. You care about people. You care about value. You care about relationships. You care about their well-being.
- What's burning inside of you is that you believe in a better present and a better future and that the people you care so much about may be veering off course. They may not even realize it, and that frustrates and motivates you to do something.
- Your story will help others open their minds to receive the signals you've perceived and empower them to embrace their own mindshift experience. They will become part of the process of creating the better future you've envisioned.

- The purpose you serve by bringing them into the cause is the realization of that future.

Now, let's go back and craft the compelling answers you have about the story you need to tell:

- Why must you tell this story?

- What's the belief burning within you that your story feeds off?

- Why will the audience leave better after your story than before they heard it?

- What greater purpose does this serve? What does it teach? What change will it inspire?

Give the WIM Exercise a Spin

Over the years, many of my friends have served as leading industry analysts at Forrester, a business and technology analyst firm that helps executives understand emergent and disruptive trends. I had the privilege to call two of them partners at Altimeter Group, Charlene Li and Jeremiah Owyang. In our early days, Charlene and Jeremiah would share lessons from their time at Forrester, where they would go through a WIM exercise. This will be of great help as you work on answering the questions above.

Think of the WIM exercise as a way of getting to the what, so what, and now what of every trend. You just keep going, level by level, uncovering what "it" means, getting deeper and deeper in the process. You're endeavoring to find deeper meaning and to counter likely arguments from the uninspired, the cynical, the naysayers, and the status quo. The goal of the WIM process is to identify meaning in each trend, who they impact and why, and what it will ultimately mean. Each layer will serve as a foundation on which to scenario plan what to do about it.

Let's take mobile UX/UI as a sample walk-through of the WIM model.

Level 1: Mobile UX/UI will introduce a new interface to consumers, one they'll have to learn.

Level 2: If this new interface is intuitive, more intuitive than traditional "point-and-click" models, consumers will inherently and subconsciously learn to prefer mobile experiences.

Level 3: If consumers prefer and expect mobile experiences, new apps and devices will build upon them to lure customers and deliver better, more seamless experiences.

Level 4: As new devices and applications succeed, customers will learn new behaviors and gain new standards for engagement and what great looks like. They will grow further and further away from traditional point-and-click, aka desktop-like services such as Web 1.0 websites, intranets, form-based applications, and mouse-driven software, and start to feel as if they are outdated.

Level 5: New technology will spur new behaviors. New technology will also reimagine processes and workflows and how people interact in their personal lives (and expect to interact at work). Once consumers feel like these experiences are outdated, they will question their loyalty to providers of these experiences, and their minds may open to providers of new, more intuitive experiences.

Level 6: As more and more consumers start to open their minds and experiment with new devices, applications, services, and new processes and workflows, hardware and software developers will look to build on this success to devise next-generation devices, applications, processes, and, ultimately, experiences. New interfaces will emerge, like voice, augmented and virtual reality, artificial intelligence, and eventually thought, which will continue to change consumer behaviors, propelling them further away from traditional products and services and business models as they seek modern, innovative, and delightful experiences.

Level 7: Companies that do not prioritize mobile UX/UI or make investments to modernize processes, workflows, services, products, or experiences and instead see it as a cost center versus growth center will eventually lose favor, loyalty, revenue, market share, and profitability. The success of innovators will not only create new experiences and opportunities for consumers; they will come at the expense of laggards who do not look inward to uncover areas to change and evolve and areas to invent and innovate.

Level 8: Those leaders who are curious, open to challenging their convention, interested in understanding how emerging trends create opportunities while also balancing existing efforts and who take insights and proactively explore internal and external cases to make improvements or create new value will find themselves on the other side of disruption. They will modernize processes, workflows, products, services, and overall experiences for employees, customers, and stakeholders, because they will have found the benefits in doing so, step-by-step, learning and growing along the way.

You now have a rough version of a story, about the future of mobile UX/UI. A good next step is to begin creating visuals that you can use to refine and share your story.

Visually Validating the What, So What, Now What (WIM) Model

As a beginning of visualizing the story that the WIM exercise has helped you begin to craft, here is a technique I've used in my work dating back to the early 2000s.

Let's start by revisiting your 2x2s from the perceive stage, which we'll use as the beginning of your visual story.

Good storytelling is rooted in believability. Visual validation is about showing people what they need to see in order to be convinced that there's something in it for them to pay attention to you, whether that's success or grave danger.

There are many visual graphs to use to show your audience the importance of the trend you're telling your story about. I'd like to share one in particular that I've become a fan of in my work because it's a highly persuasive way of showing the importance of the trend you're telling your story about. This is the spider graph, also referred to as a radar chart or star chart. This device visualizes the importance of any subject in one view, which is powerful in getting others interested in your story.

A spider graph consists of a central point and several radiating lines, in a web-like structure. The center in this case will be the trend you're telling your story about.

Each line represents a different category or variable, and the data points on each line indicate the value or score for that category. The resulting shape of the spider graph gives a visual representation of how each variable compares to the others. This is why spider graphs are often used to compare multiple sets of data in one image.[17]

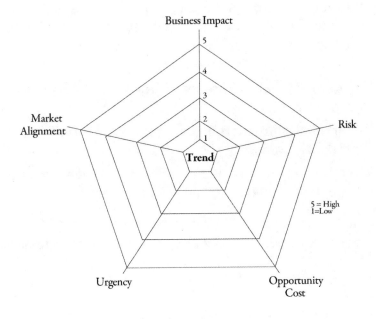

The following are the elements of a spider graph:

- **Axes:** Radiating lines that connect to the perimeter of the circle, representing each category or variable being measured
- **Axis labels:** Labels on the end of each axis that indicate what the axis represents
- **Axis scales:** The scale or range for each axis, indicating the minimum and maximum values for that category
- **Data points:** Points on each axis that indicate the value or score for that category
- **Data labels:** Labels that identify the data points and the values they represent
- **Center point:** The central point of the circle where all the axes converge

Each spider leg represents data or a category we aim to measure, which is this case are as follows:

- **Business impact:** Does this trend represent an existential threat or opportunity to our business?
- **Risk:** Is there a serious risk of investing in this trend at the expense of other priorities?
- **Opportunity cost:** What are the potential costs of not investing in this trend; i.e., will it cost us market share, share of wallet, mind share, profitability, immediately or down the line, if you miss this opportunity?
- **Urgency:** What is the sense of urgency in our need to respond now?
- **Market alignment:** Is this trend in alignment with our product roadmap?

You calculate a value score for each, and the higher the score, the further out on the radiating line you put a dot.

I created this graph about the mobile UX/UI trend. The value scale ranges from 1 to 5, with 5 representing the greatest significance.

Here's a breakdown:

- **Business impact:** Score = 3.5. Business impact is notable. As more customers become mobile first, the overall impact on the business will be even greater.

- **Risk:** Score = 1. There is almost zero risk in investing in mobile-first experiences. Customers are already mobile-first with the apps that consume their personal and professional attention. ROI is mostly certain when digital friction is removed, and the customer's experience (CX) becomes intuitive and enjoyable.

- **Opportunity cost:** Score = 3.5. Startups and competitors that invest in mobile-first experiences are attracting customers who desire a better experience. As they experiment, they are likely to proactively search for alternatives to you.

- **Urgency:** Score = 4. Every day, customers are increasingly realizing the difference between mobile-first experiences and those digital experiences where design, interaction, and transactions are largely rooted in the 1990s. It's a matter of time until they wake up to better alternatives.

- **Market alignment:** Score = 4. More devices and apps are being designed for mobile-first experiences. Multiple trends are pointing to mobile/hybrid experiences in physical spaces. The market is moving in this direction at an accelerated pace.

Here is another example, with different variables being measured:

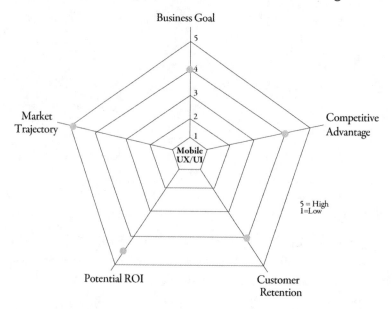

Here's a breakdown of the different variables:

- **Business goals:** Score = 4. Creating more intuitive customer experiences will increase conversions and help drive greater revenue.

- **Competitive advantage:** Score = 4. Since so many legacy companies are behind in providing mobile-first experiences, accelerating mobile-first UX/UI across the customer and employee journey will stand out.

- **Customer acquisition/retention:** Score = 4. Mobile UX/UI will give customers experiences that are intuitive and cause friction that reminds them or even introduces the idea that something better may exist elsewhere.

- **Potential ROI:** Score = 4.5. In 100% of my experiences, mobile-first pilots drive exponential growth for minimal investment. Since they're targeted at mobile users, pilots represent a relatively focused set of investments that deliver significant returns.

- **Market trajectory:** Score = 5. Technology, behavioral, and cultural trends signify that mobile is moving toward mobile-first expectations.

I have found that these spider graphs can be hugely helpful in convincing people about the urgency of disruptions I've advised them about. They've also helped me get clarity about the nature of that urgency and the story of the future I need to tell.

The Future Is Not Always Plausible

Earlier, as you underwent the WIM exercise, you were practicing one of the most potent disciplines that a futurist wields in their work: scenario planning. Here I want to address a common misconception about the nature of scenario planning. Contrary to popular belief, the job of a futurist in creating scenarios isn't to predict the future. Futurists instead describe various possibilities about how the future might unfold. Scenarios don't always represent the most predictable or probable future events. In fact, they shouldn't be limited to such. That can create complacency and foster closed-mindedness and short-termism. Good scenario planning also explores less plausible and even unlikely scenarios. By exploring multiple possibilities, including ones that we don't expect to unfold, we become more open-minded, and creative, in our exploration of the possible futures we want to depict regarding the trends we're tracking.

I learned a great deal about scenario planning from one of the leading practitioners of the art, Peter Schwartz. I can't even believe I had the opportunity to call him a colleague when we worked together at Salesforce. He's an internationally renowned futurist and business strategist and founder of the advisory group Global Business Network. One of his specialties is scenario planning, which he's done in work for the White House, the EPA, PG&E, and many other organizations. His first book, *The Art of the Long View*, is considered a seminal publication on the subject. He's also served as a script consultant on the films *The Minority Report*, *Deep Impact*, and *War Games*. He emphasizes that the purpose of scenario planning is to inform decision-making in the present. The goal is to think through the steps to take now in order to address the risks and opportunities identified in each scenario.[18]

Schwartz stresses that scenarios should consider both positive and negative outcomes, and he highlights that, in keeping with the negativity bias, "It's very easy to imagine how things might go wrong, but it's much harder to imagine how things might go right."[19] He also emphasizes that vital to useful scenarios, and at the foundation of all of your imagining, is the data you've been gathering about the trends you're tracking. As he says, "If you get your facts wrong, you get your map wrong. If you get your map wrong, you do the wrong thing." To demonstrate, he tells the cautionary tale of a shortsighted decision made by IBM.

> One of the early examples of, how shall I say, bad decision-making that shows why you need good scenario planning was a crucial decision that IBM made in 1981 about whether to go in the business of making a new product, the personal computer. And they said, "Well, look, we need to forecast demand. Is there a really big demand for this product? Is this going to be important?" And the forecast showed that it would peak at about 200,000 units and then decline pretty close to zero within a couple of years. So, this was not a very viable product. So, we'll buy the chips from Intel, we'll get the operating system from Bill Gates, and we'll put it in a box, and we'll call it an IBM PC. That was their idea. And they thought, this will last two or three years, and it'll kill off Apple. Unfortunately, they were a little wrong. It wasn't 240,000 units, it was 25,000,000. It was that failure of imagination that pointed to the need for scenarios. They needed to imagine what people could actually do when they had a bit of computing power in their hands. So, you have to have the trends, but then you also have to see the imagination about how it can change direction.[20]

So, as you think about all of the data on trends you've been gathering and possible outcomes you want to open people's minds to, be sure to really open your own mind up wide as well. Consider not only the future that seems most likely to you but also outcomes about which you might initially think, "There's no way something like that could ever happen." After all, we've been experiencing more and more black swan events as the pace of disruption has accelerated.

To help think through a wider range of possible scenarios, another good approach, combined with the WIM exercise, is to categorize them into Good, Better, Best. For each of your scenarios, you also want to assess them as Low Lift, Medium Lift, Heavy Lift, referring to how difficult they would be for your organization to address. For this evaluation of how challenging contending with a trend will be, you should next assess your organization's capabilities.

Assess Your SW><OT

You and your team possess skills and capabilities, which represent your potential or your potential risk in each scenario. Each scenario comprises opportunities and threats (OTs). How well you respond to those OTs is defined by your strengths and weaknesses (SWs). This exercise is to evaluate the strengths and weaknesses of your leadership, capabilities, skills, and operational systems and processes against possible opportunities and threats (SW >< OT).

You need to be brutally honest. The purpose is to measure the gaps between the skills and capabilities you have and those you don't. This exercise should also help you identify capabilities that you haven't known you need to have. For each scenario you develop, determine the following:

- **Assets:** List your strengths.
- **Skills needed:** List the full set of skills.
- **Assets needed:** List the capabilities you need to build.
- **Outstanding intelligence:** List the information you still need to gather.

Regarding the additional intelligence you need, good scenario planners recognize that they don't know what they don't know. So, they bring together people with different perspectives and backgrounds to share thoughts about trends. Schwartz illustrates how fruitful this was for AT&T, which he suggested talk with musician Peter Gabriel, among many others, about the digital future. As Schwartz recalls, Gabriel "brilliantly used technology to make his music. And one of the AT&T executives said, 'Peter, look they're just starting to do digital CDs...now we're gonna have lots of piracy around the world.' And he said, 'Look, I can't stop it. I know they're gonna do that. So, what I'm gonna do is treat that pirate CD as free advertising. And I'm gonna follow it with a concert. I'll make my money on the concerts, not the CDs." And that became the model in the music industry within about five years."

All of this work will be invaluable in sorting through the possibilities for the future of the trends you're tracking and crafting a compelling story about them that will shift minds. The key is to make the scenarios you craft pragmatic and relatable even if the future you portray seems implausible. This is also why you next want to work on telling a compelling story about the scenarios. You want to bring them to vivid life through your storytelling, which will be the trendspark that ignites a communal mindshift.

The Future As We Want It to Be

As these exercises have shown, weaving our findings together to create our story can be taxing. It's important as you dive into this exploration that you make time to give your brain a rest and have some fun. So, let me close this chapter with a little discussion about one of the greatest stories ever told.

Douglas Adams was reportedly penniless when he conceived the idea for the blockbuster radio series, then book, *The Hitchhiker's Guide to the Galaxy*. That all changed to say the least!

It's said that when Adams was touring Europe, he had in hand a copy of *The Hitchhiker's Guide to Europe*. One night, while looking at the stars, perhaps a bit inspired by imbibing,[21] he came up with the idea of exploring the galaxy from a hitchhiker's perspective.

Anyone who loves the story knows the number 42. It's the stuff of legend.

But what does it mean?

42 is the answer to the "ultimate question of life, the universe, and everything."

The actor Stephen Fry claimed Adams shared its meaning, but said he'll take the secret to his grave. There are many theories, with Adams himself saying that the answer was a joke. Adams told the story this way[22]:

> "It had to be a number, an ordinary, smallish number, and I chose that one...sat on my desk, stared into the garden and thought 42 will do. I typed it out. End of story."

Is that the end of the story? Maybe. But one theory I quite like goes like this: in the story, we're introduced to a great supercomputer called Deep Thought, the most powerful computer ever built, designed by hyper-intelligent pan-dimensional beings. These super beings wanted to know the answer to "Life, the Universe, and Everything."[23]

The answer was, "42."

To understand the meaning of the answer is to understand the times when the story was developed. The year was 1979. Computers at the time were programmed using American Standard Code for Information Interchange (ASCII).[24] In ASCII, 42 represents an asterisk (*) or "wildcard" for programmers to take control of what happens next.[25] Some have therefore argued that 42 is saying that the meaning of life is to take control of what happens next.[26]

Translated, Deep Thought solved the age-old riddle, based on its infinite wisdom, with an answer that's as simple as it is profound, "Life is what you make it." Said another way, life is anything you want it to be.

The same is true for the future. Since it hasn't happened yet, you can have an incredible influence on it, or should I say *trendfluence*. And that leads us to the next step in crafting our story.

Chapter 10

Conceive

As you now consider how to craft a story out of all of the information you've gathered and all of your thinking through of scenarios, remind yourself that many of those in your audience will know little about the trends you're discussing. You have to excite their interest in them. Also be alert that they'll be listening to your story through the filters of their respective points of view, including biases, self-interests, and pressures they're under.

They need to hear a story that is aware and respectful of what's important to them, what they value, the goals and deliverables they're measured against, and what can help them thrive. Otherwise, you may be treated as the proverbial "bearer of bad news." Stay mindful that visions of disruptive change make many people uncomfortable, even when the opportunities they describe seem undeniably compelling to you.

Remember that stories release the "love hormone" oxytocin in the brain? Well, the scientist who discovered that, Paul J. Zak, also found that if a story feels threatening, it will release a different hormone in the brain, cortisol. This is the "fight-or-flight hormone," which leads us to react defensively and causes stress, whether that's in response to a physical threat or to information we find discomforting. If people feel threatened by your story, their walls will go up, and they might respond badly. They might even seek to retaliate against you in various ways.

While I was writing this chapter, I was struck by this image portraying the challenges faced by those who design digital products, known as user experience (UX) designers.[1] The FAANG reference in the image refers to the five, at least then, best-performing tech companies of the past decade, Facebook (now Meta), Apple, Netflix, and Google. They're like the *Wonderful World of Oz* for UX designers. This is a great example of telling a story efficiently with an image. The story told represents a dilemma we all face when we're seeking to drive disruptive change. Do we do what's best or what's best for us?

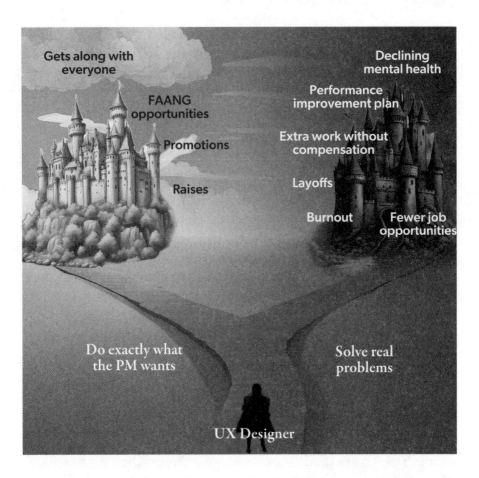

On one side, if we give in and follow the status quo, we become part of the machine, a factory that churns out work based on yesterday's experiences and the strategies they dictate. This can put us in good political standing, helping us to earn raises, promotions, and career growth.

On the other side, if we aim to solve real problems, fix what's broken, see alternative paths toward progress, innovate and unlock new value, and take risks, we may face an incredible array of negative consequences. This is because, though we're trying to do what's right, we are challenging the status quo, a deeply guarded sanctuary of how people choose to live and work. Even though what's on the other side of change or progress can be more rewarding, it can be easier to excel within the confines of convention and is definitely more comfortable.

This is why truth tellers, forecasters of the future, and visionaries always struggle to get some of those who should be receptive to their insights to pay them heed.[2] That's true even when a disruption foreseen, or even already underway, potentially spells doom.

Psychologists have identified the tendency to ignore or knowingly dismiss a prediction of a crisis as a common psychological phenomenon, which they call the Cassandra complex.[3] The name comes from the story of Cassandra in Greek mythology, who was the daughter of Priam, the king who reigned Troy at the time when Greeks attacked. Her beauty attracted the attention of the God Apollo, the son of Zeus. As a token of his love, he bestowed the gift of prophecy upon her. But she refused his offering, which enraged him. In response, Apollo cursed Cassandra to prophesize the truth and also suffer from knowing no one would believe her.

Warren Buffett referenced the tale when he testified before Congress about the 2008 financial crisis. He referred to the prophetic "big short" investor Michael Burr as having been treated like Cassandra when he issued stark, and accurate, warnings of the impending market crash.[4] Burr was not only vindicated, of course, but he made a fortune, for himself and his investment clients, by shorting the crash. Unfortunately, many of those who take the risk of sharing visions of future disruption face instead the kinds of troubles that our UX designer sees before him. That is why telling a great story, one that unlocks minds and sparks a mindshift, is so important. If we deliver a story of the future in a way that makes people excited or motivated, suddenly our vision is a boon. We're now the bearer of good news! And we inspire those who might work against us to support us.

Keeping the Cassandra complex in mind as we work on developing our story is of great help. Assuming we will be met by resistance helps motivate us to put the work in to weave a more relatable, compelling, and inclusive story. This does take some real work, because telling such stories is a delicate art. Yes, you're learning an art form. After all, you're not aiming for a good story, you want to tell a great one.

Essential Elements of a Great Story

These are tips for a great story:

Great stories are relevant and relatable

Your audience will care more about stories that include people, places, and things that are familiar to them and are important to them.[5] Your audience should feel like they see themselves in the story. This is called narrative proximity. The goal is that they see themselves as the heroes you need them to be.

Great stories appeal to our deepest emotions

For the most part, there are six basic emotions that we're working with: anger, disgust, fear, happiness, sadness, and surprise.[6] There are others of course, but these are the most powerful. You want to work with them because the stronger the emotion, the more compelling the response. Being immersive and vivid, your story will help your audience feel the importance of your story. Is it a matter of survival? Is it a threat to the business or their role? Is there an upside to this trend where the audience becomes a hero? You want them absorbed!

Great stories are both perosnal and universal

You want to draw on both compelling, personal experiences and ones that have a universal quality so you can connect your experience with those in your audience.

Great stories have a character to root for

We tend to admire a character more for trying than for their success. This is why so many of us love to cheer for the underdog. When we root for a character, we're in effect going on their journey with them. They become a hero, and their quest becomes our quest.[7]

Great stories introduce something unanticipated

They make the unexpected a curiosity trigger.[8] Surprising the audience makes your story compelling. It's also how we learn new things. The trick is to make the unexpected not only interesting but also insightful. You're helping your audience experience something new and grow as a result.

Great stories make you care about how they will end

When you are engrossed in a story and the chapter of the book or the episode of the show ends without conclusion, you're compelled to turn the page to the next chapter or to binge the next episode. This is the power of cliffhangers; they bait the audience into hanging on for the next part of the story.

Great stories have a compelling narrative arc

They are structured in a way that engages the audience in trying to figure out what will happen. With the best stories, we're not passively sitting back and just letting the story unfold; we're wondering what will come next. We're trying to anticipate the turns the story will take. How is the hero going to get out of this fix!

Crafting a story with all of these elements is a tall order, which is why in this chapter, we'll turn to some of the world's greatest experts on the art of storytelling to offer their sage advice about how to develop your story.

Connecting Trends to the Human Condition by Making Your Story Personal

If a story is to bring us together in a shared mindshift, to tackle the future in a way we can all believe in and rally around, we must connect trends to the things that matter in people's live. We must make our story personal, both to ourselves and to them. This makes stories meaningful and motivating.

Robert McKee is an award-winning writer and director, described by *Harvard Business Review* as "the world's best-known and most respected screenwriting lecturer."[9] He taught screenwriting and storytelling at the University of Southern California's School of Cinema and Television before forming his own company, Two-Arts. McKee is also the author of the seminal book on storytelling, *Story: Substance, Structure, Style, and the Principles of Screenwriting*. He writes that stories "fulfill a profound human need to grasp the patterns of living— not merely as an intellectual exercise, but within a very personal, emotional experience."[10]

We want our audience to feel not only immersed in the story, but as if they're a character in it. To do this, we have to put some of ourselves into the story. We have to draw on our own experiences to invest the story with the emotion that will draw our audience in.

Recall that acclaimed director Pete Docter advises that we write about events in our lives that made us feel some particular way.[11] He recounts how he drew on his personal experience in order to achieve this in creating the story of *Monsters, Inc.*

While Docter humbly describes himself as a "geeky kid from Minnesota who likes to draw cartoons,"[12] he is one of the most successful storytellers of our time, having been nominated for four Oscars and winning three for best animated feature,[13] the only person in history to have done so. He emphasizes that any story, to truly connect with someone, has to be rooted in personal experiences because that's what makes them relatable. Trends that are described as forces at work out in the world, but not in terms of how they will affect us in our daily lives, will not be captivating. Drawing on our daily life experiences and how a trend might affect us will help us to then convince others about how the trend may affect them.

We might think that the story of *Monsters, Inc.* would have immediately grabbed anyone. It's the story of a monster who scares kids for a living. It's funny just to type this. As Docter describes the story in brief, the monster clocks into work, eats donuts, pays his union dues, terrifies kids, and then clocks out for the day.[14]

I mean, that sounds like a great story.

But Docter found that when he and his team tested the story in film, viewers got bored. At the time, Docter was expecting his first child, and he realized that he could invest the story with some of the emotion he was feeling. He could make it more moving if he considered it as the story of his journey into fatherhood, and into the unknown. "What I finally figured out was that it's not actually about a monster who scares kids, it's about a man becoming a father."

This understanding opened the dams for Docter to pour his heart, fears, and aspirations into the story. It was no longer a story about monsters who clocked in and out at work to scare children. It was about caring, attachment, not losing one's identity, and also about becoming the opposite of a monster.

To help bring trends and scenarios to life, Docter suggests that we reflect on the moments in our life, or those who matter to us, when we or they experienced big events, full of emotion. Always remember that storytelling is most influential when you spark the emotions of your audience.

Robin McKee also stresses pulling from our own lives. "Self-knowledge is the root of all great storytelling," McKee writes. "A storyteller creates all characters from the self by asking the question, 'If I were this character in these circumstances, what would I do?' The more you understand your own humanity, the more you can appreciate the humanity of others in all their good-versus-evil struggles."[15]

Those struggles are the next source you want to draw on in crafting your story. This is how you can make your story not only personal, but universal.

The Best Stories Are About the Human Condition We All Share

The specific details of your story should relate to universal themes of human life because these themes connect with the interests, biases, and aspirations of your audience. They include the following:

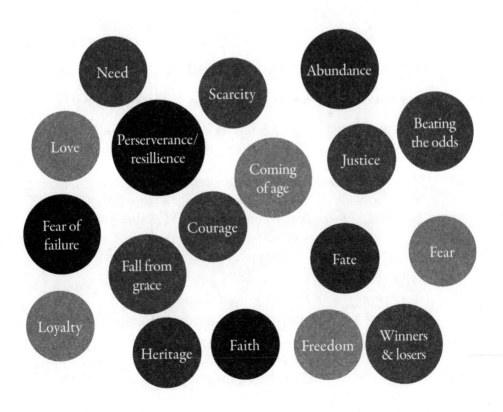

Consider how you might tell a story about a trend in a way that shows how that trend can help your audience with these universal aspects of our lives. How might the trend relate to one or more of these everyday challenges and goals of your audience? How might an emerging trend allow them to strengthen their relationships with their loved ones? How might it help them beat the odds of getting a big promotion? How might it help them build up their resilience?

To do this, step into their shoes. What is their reality? What are their fears? What does success look like to them? Now, think again about how the trend might either enhance their reality or make it more difficult. The following are good questions to ask:

Because of this trend…

…what might we lose?

…what might we gain?

…what might we learn?

…how might we win?

…how could we surpass our competitors?

…how could we change our course to avoid x or gain y?

McKee advises that as we do this delving into the needs and desires of our audience we ask these additional key questions[16]:

- What does my protagonist want in order to restore balance in his or her life? "Desire is the blood of a story," McKee believes. "Desire is…a core need that, if satisfied, would stop the story in its tracks."

- What is keeping my protagonist from achieving their desire? Is it forces within? Is it doubt? Fear? Confusion? Anxiety? Is it emerging conflicts with co-workers, teams, employees, partners? Is it looming market disruption as a result of emerging trends? Is it internal and external conflicts arising in the various institutions in society that affect our markets? Not enough time to get things done or effectively prepare? Don't have the ability or the resources to assess and respond to trends? Is it executives or a board that doesn't "get it" and is holding you back? "Antagonists come from people, society, time, space, and every object in it, or any combination of these forces at once," McKee states.

- How should your protagonist decide to act in order to achieve their desire in the face of these antagonistic forces? "It's in the answer to that question that storytellers discover the truth of their characters, because the heart of a human being is revealed in the choices he or she makes under pressure," McKee shares.

- Now, take a step back and rehearse the scenario out loud and ask yourself, do I believe this? Ask yourself, is this a correct and realistic representation of the human condition, of likely scenarios that may lead to disruption? Is it sensationalized? Is it underrepresented? Is this an honest telling?

If you are convinced that this proto-story you've been developing meets those criteria, it's time to move on to shaping your story.

If It Sounds Too Good to Be True, There's Something Wrong with the Plot

Every great story is told through a compelling storyline, in other words, the plot. This underlying structure of your story pulls your audience in and carries them along through a series of scenes that put them through an experience, a journey. This is often referred to as the *hero's journey*. Your goal is to make your audience put themselves in the place of the hero and the supporting characters as they face challenges and, ultimately, triumph. The best plots are simple while also full of drama.

Here is a simple plot that you could begin with:

Once upon a time…

Important trends were taking shape…

Which meant, the hero had to…

But the hero faced…

If the hero didn't act or inspire action, what would happen next could spell the…

That's when the hero…

Others realized they too needed to become the heroes they were waiting for…

Then what they learned unlocked…

And they lived happily ever after.

You can also draw on the long history of great stories to start with a basic story type that's worked through the ages.

Story experts agree that there is a finite set of great story plots. Here I present a set of the most common ones. The one that most aligns with the culture of your organization, or the behaviors of your team, can help you tell your story in just the right way. Consider how trends paired with the corresponding plot type tell the most compelling story.[17]

- **The quest:** Frame the impending disruption as a quest or journey, where your company's success depends on embarking on a new path. Highlight the challenges and opportunities that lie ahead, emphasizing the need for transformation.

- **Overcoming the monster:** Present the disruptive trend as a formidable monster or threat that your company must face. Showcase the potential consequences of inaction and illustrate how your proposed changes can vanquish the monster and lead to success.

- **Rags to riches:** Tell a story of a company's transformation from a struggling or stagnant state to a flourishing one. Illustrate how embracing the disruptive trend can help your organization rise above the competition and achieve unprecedented success.

- **The underdog:** Paint your company as the underdog, facing powerful competitors or market forces. Highlight how the disruptive trend can level the playing field and provide unique opportunities for your organization to excel against all odds.

- **Rebirth:** Illustrate a narrative of rebirth and renewal for your company. Show how embracing the disruptive trend can breathe new life into your organization, revitalizing its purpose, culture, and performance.

- **Comedy:** Use humor and wit to convey the need for change. Frame the disruptive trend as a comedic situation that requires your company's innovative response. Engage your audience through laughter while delivering a compelling message about the importance of adaptation.

- **Tragedy:** Craft a story that demonstrates the potential downfall or loss your company may face if it fails to address the disruptive trend. Show the dire consequences of resisting change and emphasize the urgency of taking action to avoid tragedy.

Pixar on What If?

To start developing the specifics of your story, making it original and distinctive, you can't do better than to now go through the exercise Pixar always begins with in developing their stories. Pixar starts with a simple but powerful question, "what if"?

The company introduces about this in an online storytelling course through the Khan Academy.[18] In a video, Pixar storytellers share the following:

> "Although our movies involve hundreds of people and take years to make, they all begin with a simple idea about some world and character.
>
> **What if there's life out there in the universe?**
>
> **What if a rat wanted to cook haute cuisine?**
>
> **What if our toys that are all around us actually were sentient and can come alive?**
>
> These what-if questions invite the imagination into a story we want to explore.
>
> What ifs help us understand directions our story could take. They help us spin out various scenarios, and that helps us narrow down what's most important to our audience and ultimately what can be left on the cutting-room floor.

- What if this new trend disrupts my business or work?

- What if this trend gave us a new superpower?

- What if customers change because of this trend, and how might we take advantage of it?

- What if our leaders forecast this trend well in advance and used it to enhance the capabilities of our workforce?

- What if this new trend unlocked the ability to empower workers to deliver 10x output?

Pixar also notes that "what if" statements are "ultimately connected to a world and a character." The world might be our market, our HQ or office, our customer's world, etc. Characters may include not only the hero but others who will play a role in bringing this trend and its effects to life. Effective storytelling is premised on how well our audience gets to know these characters and how relatable and influential they become.

Engage with the Story Spine

Another great exercise for developing your story was created by playwright and actor Kenn Adams. He calls it the *story spine*.[19] He originally used it in teaching people about improvisational theater, but it's been adopted since for developing all sorts of stories.[20] Adams describes it as "an eight-sentence exercise that helps us learn and practice how good stories are told."[21] The story spine provides the beginning of the sentences, and you fill in the rest.

> **Once upon a time there was ____. Every day, ____. One day ____. Because of that, ____. Because of that, ____. Because of that. _____ Until finally ____. And Ever Since Then _____.**
>
> **With the optional added line to fill in: And the moral of the story is._____**

Adams illustrates how the story spine can help create a great story by using it to summarize the plots of popular movies.[22] Here, I'll use a Pixar example since this is a Pixar-themed chapter.

The Story Spine
The simple foundations of many stories

BEGINING
1. Once upon a time...

2. Every day...

THE EVENT
3. But, one day...

MIDDLE
4. Because of that...

5. Because of that...

6. Because of that...

THE CLIMAX
7. Until finally...

END
8. And, ever since then...

OPTIONAL
And, the moral of
the story is...

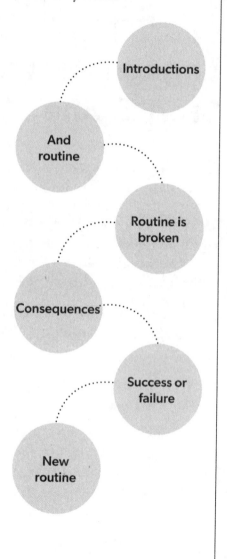

The Incredibles

Once upon a time, there was a superhero named Mr. Incredible who was forced to live as an ordinary man in a society where superheroes were outlawed.

Every day, he grew more and more frustrated with his stifling, boring life.

But one day, he accepted a secret superhero job from a mysterious stranger.

Because of that, he fell into the diabolical trap of this mysterious stranger who turned out to be Syndrome, a super villain with a long-time grudge against Mr. Incredible.

Because of that, Syndrome was able to capture and imprison Mr. Incredible.

Because of that, Syndrome could now put his master plan into motion by setting a giant, killer-robot loose on civilization.

Until finally, Mr. Incredible escaped from his prison and foiled the villain by destroying the giant, killer-robot.

And ever since then, he was loved by all and able to be a superhero again.

The Hero's Journey

Another great preconceived storyline that you can use for developing your story is the hero's journey popularized by Joseph Campbell. It's been the inspiration for some of the most successful movie storylines of all time including *Star Wars*, *The Lion King*, *The Matrix*, *Indiana Jones*, *and Harry Potter*. It's also inspired many other movies, books, albums, and plays.

Campbell introduced the journey in his epic 1949 book, *The Hero with a Thousand Faces*.[23] He saw the hero's journey as a universal motif of adventure and transformation that, in his research, runs through virtually all the world's mythic traditions.

The Swiss psychologist Carl Jung also believed in the idea of such universal "archetypes,"[24] which, he said, appear in the dreams of all people and the myths of all cultures. This is thought to be why the hero's journey is such a powerful narrative arc.

Campbell broke the hero's journey down into 12 steps in three acts. You might want to draw on some elements of it and not others, tailoring it to the needs of your story.

I'll introduce the steps of the journey with some notation about how they can apply to crafting your story about the threats and opportunities of the trends you're focusing on. I'll also include, in italics, references to popular movies that drew on elements of the journey, which were crafted by Christopher Vogler when he was working as a story consultant at Disney in the 1980s. As a student of cinema at the University of Southern California, Vogler theorized that George Lucas had drawn on the hero's journey in creating the first Star Wars movie, and he wrote a term paper making that case. While working for Disney, Vogler decided to dig into how elements of the journey contributed to the power of other great movies as well.[25] He flew to New York to work with his good friend David McKenna on the exploration, recalling that they "wore out his VCR looking at old movie clips."

After Vogler shared a seven-page summary of their findings with Disney executives, it started to circulate and generate buzz at studios all across Hollywood. Vogler recalls:

> "I heard young executives buzzing about it, telling their friends about it. It became the 'I have to have it;' document of the season at talent agencies and in studio executive suites. Jeffrey Katzenberg [then one of those Disney executives] pronounced it a very important document at a meeting of his development execs, making it required reading for the entire staff."

Katzenberg offered Vogler a position in Disney's Feature Animation division, where they worked on *The Lion King*. "When I arrived, I found the memo had preceded me, and the animators were already outlining their storyboards with hero's journey stages," Vogler recalled.

Hero's Journey Overview Featuring Vogler's Commentary from The Memo

Act 1:
The Ordinary World/The Departure[26]

We're introduced to the hero who lives in their "ordinary world." Before long, the hero receives a call to adventure. The hero is unsure or reticent to follow this call, which is referred to as the "refusal of the call." However, the hero is then greeted by a mentor figure, who offers counsel and convinces him to follow the call.

In your story, the mentor is you, and the hero is representative of the people you're hoping to motivate.

1. **Ordinary world:** Your hero is working in a new normal, working in their version of business as usual.

   In STAR WARS you see Luke Skywalker being bored to death as a farm boy before he tackles the universe.

2. **Call to adventure:** The hero is presented with the threats and opportunities inherent in the trendscape canvas.

   Maybe the land is dying, as in the King Arthur stories about the search for the Grail. In STAR WARS, it's Princess Leia's holographic message to Obi Wan Kenobi, who then asks Luke to join the quest. In detective stories, it's the hero being offered a new case.

3. **Refusal of the call:** Fears, doubt, cynicism, arrogance, and ignorance stand in the way of transformation and progress. They seem overwhelming and insurmountable.

   Luke refuses Obi Wan's call to adventure and returns to his aunt and uncle's farmhouse, only to find they have been barbecued by the emperor's stormtroopers. Suddenly Luke is no longer reluctant and is eager to undertake the adventure.

4. **Meeting the mentor:** This is you! This also represents the experts and data and supporting material you offer to guide our hero.

   In JAWS it's the crusty Robert Shaw character who knows all about sharks. The mentor gives advice and sometimes magical weapons. This is Obi Wan giving Luke his father's light saber. The mentor can go only so far with the hero. Eventually, the hero must face the unknown by himself. Sometimes the Wise Old Man/Woman is required to give the hero a swift kick in the pants to get the adventure going.

5. **Crossing the threshold:** Convinced, the hero is ready to act, to step out of their comfort zone to interrogate the future, to explore the unknown, and to embrace their calling.

   This is the moment at which the story takes off and the adventure gets going. The balloon goes up, the romance begins, the spaceship blasts off, the wagon train gets rolling. Dorothy sets out on the Yellow Brick Road. The hero is now committed to their journey and there's no turning back.

Act 2:
The Special World/The Initiation

In this phase, the hero enters a "special world," where they begin their quest to tackle the challenge before them and transform. They're met with a series of tasks that take them on their journey until they reach the climax of the story—the main obstacle (the trend, the disruption, the impact). Here, the hero must put into practice everything they've learned on their journey to overcome the obstacle (the mindshift). The hero gains accolades, but also experience and wisdom.

1. **Tests, allies, enemies:** The hero is confronted by the challenges they once feared or ignored. Obstacles are thrown across their path. It's also how the hero grows wiser and stronger while also giving them experiences that build character and leadership. Along the way they encounter new allies to help them in their journey.

   In STAR WARS, the cantina is the setting for the forging of an important alliance with Han Solo and the start of an important enmity with Jabba the Hutt. In CASABLANCA, Rick's Café is the setting for the "alliances and enmities" phase and in many Westerns it's the saloon where these relationships are tested.

2. **Approach to the inmost cave:** The tests up to this point lead the hero deep into their journey, beyond the point of no return as they tackle the meaning and opportunities inherent in the trendscape canvas. As the hero approaches this stage, they must muster the courage to take the final step into the unknown, to face their fears, and to understand the secrets to transformation and progress.

   In the Arthurian stories the Chapel Perilous is the dangerous chamber where the seeker finds the Grail. In STAR WARS it's Luke and company being sucked into the Death Star where they will rescue Princess Leia. Sometimes it's just the hero going into their own dream world to confront fears and overcome them.

3. **Ordeal:** The "supreme ordeal" represents the actual change in thinking, the changes in behavior, and the unlearning and unraveling of old ways and embracing the new learnings and routines needed to move forward.

   In STAR WARS, it's the harrowing moment in the bowels of the Death Star where Luke, Leia, and company are trapped in the giant trash-masher. Luke is pulled under by the tentacled monster that lives in the sewage and is held down so long that the audience begins to wonder if he's dead. In E.T., THE EXTRATERRESTRIAL, E.T. momentarily appears to die on the operating table. This is a critical moment in any story, an ordeal in which the hero appears to die and be born again.

It's a major source of the magic of the hero myth. What happens is that the audience has been led to identify with the hero. We are encouraged to experience the brink-of-death feeling with the hero. We are temporarily depressed, and then we are revived by the hero's return from death.

4. **Reward (seizing the sword):** After facing their greatest challenges, the hero is transformed into a new state, a stronger, more confident, and capable leader, with the reward of gaining the experience of leading transformation and progress and the ability to face their next challenge.

   The hero now takes possession of the treasure he's come seeking. Sometimes it's a special weapon like a magic sword, or it may be a token like the Grail or some elixir that can heal the wounded land. The hero may settle a conflict with his father or with his shadowy nemesis. In RETURN OF THE JEDI, Luke is reconciled with both, as he discovers that the dying Darth Vader is his father and not such a bad guy after all.

5. **The road back:** The path back to their new normal is one that faces acclaim and vindication, and perhaps even exoneration.[27] The skeptics and cynics and naysayers and those who hem and haw, non-conformists, and nonbelievers now see what success looks like on the other side. Now the hero must choose between their own personal objectives and those of a higher purpose.

   Some of the best chase scenes come at this point, as the hero is pursued by the vengeful forces from whom he has stolen the elixir or the treasure. This is the chase as Luke and friends are escaping from the Death Star, with Princess Leia and the plans that will bring down Darth Vader.

Act 3:
The Return to the Ordinary World

Now that the hero has faced and overcome the challenge, they are ready to return to the new normal they've helped to shape. Once back, though, things are hardly normal. There's a keen awareness that things are new. They're appreciated as such, but now a receiver's state is activated. The hero is always paying attention to what lies ahead, and they become the mentor, the leader, to help others always.

1. **Resurrection:** This is the climax, which presents the final test, the final battle. This could be the strong urge to settle in a new normal. It can be the threat of complacency. The final test could represent saboteurs who want things to go back to the old ways. Without backing down, our hero commits to their higher purpose and returns as a person reborn, a new leader for a new era.

   There is often a replay here of the mock death-and-rebirth of Stage 8, as the hero once again faces death and survives. The Star Wars movies play with this theme constantly—all of the films to date feature a final battle scene in which Luke is almost killed, appears to be dead for a moment, and then miraculously survives. He is transformed into a new being by his experience.

2. **Return with the elixir:** Returning to their ordinary world, the hero arrives as a changed person. They've grown. They're ready to start their new life. Doubters are ostracized. Enemies are penalized and allies rewarded. As a leader, they share their wisdom, experiences, and lessons to help others also lead. Our hero is ready for their next calling.

   Sometimes it's just knowledge or experience, but unless he comes back with the elixir or some boon to mankind, he's doomed to repeat the adventure until he does. Many comedies use this ending, as a foolish character refuses to learn his lesson and embarks on the same folly that got him in trouble in the first place. Sometimes the boon is treasure won on the quest, or love, or just the knowledge that the special world exists and can be survived. Sometimes it's just coming home with a good story to tell.

As you think about how you might use some elements of the hero's journey to make your mindshifting story powerful, remember that in asking those you're working to persuade to join in your cause, they're going to need you to be their Obi-Wan Kenobi, their Yoda, their Dumbledore, their Abner Ravenwood (Indiana Jones). That's a tall order, I know. But as you've been reading this book, you've been going on your own hero's journey, which is preparing you to be that guide.

The mindshift journey I've been taking you on started by inviting you on a call to adventure. I depicted the refusal of the call—not by you, but by the naysayers and hem-hawers. I've introduced you to a host of mentors, and I've hoped to be a mentor myself. In the last few chapters, as you've worked on identifying trends and evaluating the story to tell about them, you've crossed the threshold into becoming a leader who will inspire others to mindshift.

You are learning to be the hero who leads the way for them. Or, as Brad Montague, author of *Becoming Better Grownups*, says the leader who shows others that the world "pulses with possibilities."[28] You're learning the tools you need to be he hero leader you wish you had and that others need you to be.[29]

The next step in making your story persuasive is to begin sketching it out, and the best way to do that is to storyboard it.

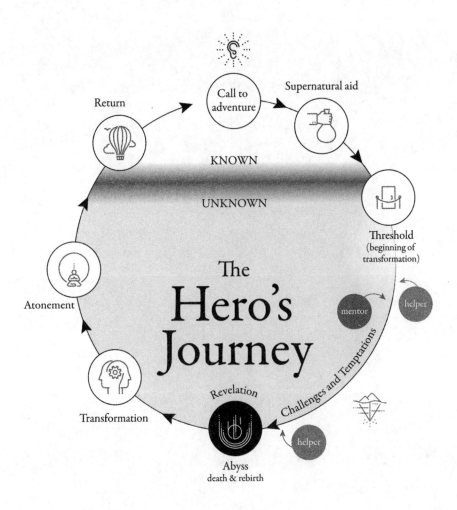

The

Hero's Journey

Return

Call to adventure

Supernatural aid

KNOWN

UNKNOWN

Threshold
(beginning of
transformation)

Atonement

mentor

helper

Challenges and Temptations

Transformation

Revelation

helper

Abyss
death & rebirth

Chapter 11

Believe

The Power of Storyboarding

You can't catalyze a mindshift unless your story is relatable and convincing. In cinematic storytelling, for which storyboarding was invented, the popular term for this is *believability*. In believable stories, the audience identifies with the characters and finds the situations they're in, the challenges they're facing, the emotions they're feeling, and the actions they take credible.

Believability is the driving factor in inspiring people to embrace your vision for change and then help you champion it. If your story isn't believable, it will raise objections in your audience as their logical minds take charge and poke holes in the case you're making. As we'll explore more in the next chapter, inspiring people to take action requires you to convince both people's hearts and heads. Storyboarding is the way to make sure your story has this power.

> Storyboards are a way of prototyping human experience. They allow us to imagine, critique, and iterate possibilities for our characters and how their story will unfold."
>
> —Nick Sung

Most simply, a storyboard is a series of sketches that maps out a story. Each sketch depicts a key moment in your story, which I call *story beats*. Creating boards helps focus on what those moments should be in order for your story to elicit your desired audience reaction.

The process was invented by animators at the Walt Disney company, and it was vital in making their first feature-length film, *Snow White and the Seven Dwarfs*. It helped them improve the story, testing ideas for scenes and how characters would look and act before doing the arduous, and expensive, work of the actual animation. As two of Disney's character animators wrote in their book *The Illusion of Life*, they learned that they could create a story that was more than just entertaining but was actually deeply moving.

Storyboarding first helps you empathize with the people who are represented by the characters in your story. It enables you to understand details of experiences people are having, or can have in the future, that you want to help them with. Then it helps you to evoke that empathy in your audience by figuring out how best to portray what your characters are going through to people who may never have had those experiences.

I studied the Disney way of storyboarding and storytelling for years, and in 2012, I was introduced to the work of Nick Sung, a former storyboard artist at Pixar. He's worked on many of their great films, including *Up*, *Ratatouille*, and *Toy Story 3*. He shared that "Storyboards are a way of prototyping human experience. They allow us to imagine, critique, and iterate possibilities for our characters and how their story will unfold." They help hone in on specific moments of your characters' experience to illuminate. As Nick says, "Over time, the process forces us to zoom from the big picture to the telling moments to the fine details." By visualizing those essential moments, boards allow your audience to actually feel the experience of them.

Let's say that you're trying to communicate to your audience the challenges that someone who is confined to a wheelchair faces in navigating your office space. Your goal is to get management to make a number changes in the space to improve your colleague's daily work experience. You could tell the management about the problems, or you could show someone going through those difficulties, viscerally compelling your audience to put themselves within your story and to see and feel the difficulties much as your colleague does. This is the power of storyboarding.

When I was working with one of the biggest U.S. retailers, executives were concerned with offering better omnichannel customer experiences. To my delight, they showed me a series of visualizations that portrayed two well-studied, organized, and articulated customer journeys, one online and the other in-store. But they hadn't created any scenes of customers actually going through the journeys. They hadn't portrayed any of the emotions customers might feel, or thoughts they'd be having, as they shopped. Their visualizations also didn't capture differences in the journeys that customers would likely experience due to having different shopping styles and preferences. They had portrayed one general customer experience.

I worked with the team to visualize a range of experiences of different customers, creating storyboards that visualized specific experiences based on the different behaviors, aspirations, and goals of real shoppers. We did this for all of the following shopping scenarios:

- Mobile-first shopping (app for on-demand delivery services)
- Online shipping (home delivery using shipping service)
- Shopping in store with a mobile device
- Self-checkout
- Line checkout
- BOPIS (buy online and pickup in store)
- Curbside
- Parking
- In-store list shopping

I can't reveal all of the discoveries we made, but let's consider differences for two shopper characters we profiled, based on my trendscaping research about omnichannel retail.

Molly

She's mobile-first, a heavy TikTok and Instagram user, who clocks at least four hours of screen time per day. She enjoys the incredibly personalized advertising she sees in her feed on social media, even though she knows her devices are listening to and tracking her activity (as long as ads and offers stay relevant!). She works faster than typical customers on her devices. For example, she listens to podcasts and watches YouTube videos at 1.2 or 1.5 speed, and she uses ChatGPT to provide short summaries of long articles and reviews.

If Molly were shopping in store, she would be glued to her phone most of the time, checking reviews of items on TikTok and comparing prices with other retailers. She most likely would opt for an app to arrange delivery. A second option would be to buy online and pick up in store.

John

He's an in-store shopper who comes in only for what he needs, but he is open to interesting promotions he might see as he walks through the store. John uses a smartphone, but not for shopping. For him, his phone is for email, texting, web browsing, listening to music, and playing games, like his favorite, Wordle. He's not constantly checking it, and he doesn't keep up with all the hot new apps. Sometimes he needs to ask family and friends for tech support.

One set of storyboards showed Molly breezing through the store for her items and effortlessly using a new self-checkout process, which allowed her to cut out 10 minutes from her shopping time that she didn't have to spend waiting in line. She is delighted, and she uses that time to grab a latte at her favorite coffee boutique.

In considering the boards, executives noted that Molly didn't pay attention to end caps or point-of-purchase displays, helping them understand what a different kind of shopper she was from the traditional brick-and-mortar customer. They also observed that she wasn't using the retail app as it was designed to be used, for remote shopping. She helped them understand that it could also be an effective channel for in-store shopping and for all-around engagement with their brand.

Another set of boards showed John shopping. He starts off by heading at a good clip to the sporting goods area. But then he stops at a display of batteries on sale and picks up a pack to buy. After then finding the athletic stocks he came for, he decides to try self-checkout because the line for the register is long. He struggles with the self-checkout process and asks for assistance. Waiting five minutes for someone to come, he gets increasingly annoyed and considers leaving without making his purchases. As he walks out of the store, a thought bubble reads, "What a pain! Why would they put in self-checkouts and not hire more checkers for the registers!?"

While the executives were pleased to see confirmation of the value of their continued in-store promotions, they were appropriately dismayed by the dismal experience John had with self-checkout.

Developing such specific profiles of characters for your story and then envisioning them going through an experience helps you set aside your personal beliefs and experiences and empathize with all sorts of other people who may have very different beliefs and experiences than you. You, for example, might absolutely love any and all new technologies, like Molly. So, you might not be empathetic to John, thinking he's just a luddite, until you create boards depicting his frustration.

I was reminded the other day about how instructive storyboarding was when I became frustrated myself while shopping. The self-checkout line went back into the aisles, so I decided to stand in line for a checker. I distracted myself in the time spent in line by scrolling through my favorite apps. But even so, I got annoyed by how long the wait was, and I looked up to see what was taking so long. A customer at one of the registers was using cash for a large purchase and was fumbling through her wallet for exact bills and change. At one point, she emptied her change purse out on the counter to find what she needed. She then gave up counting change and pulled out another bill. "Ugh!" I thought, only to smile to myself. Though I'm not the age of the typical mobile-first consumer like Molly, I sure can act like one!

The fact is that empathizing with those who prefer to shop differently from us can be quite difficult. This is true for any experience businesses offer. This is why when I show storyboards of such customer experiences to executives they commonly respond, "I had no idea!"

I can't show you the storyboards I created for that retailer, so to explore further how useful they are and how to create them, let me share some that were created by Nick Sung, who's much more accomplished than me in the craft.

Mindshifting
the Pixar Way

One of Nick's projects was to help Airbnb envision the future of its host and guest experiences. I described that work in my book, *X: The Experience When Business Meets Design*. In fact, Nick helped me with storyboarding that book, and the process made me rethink the book completely.

I'll tell the story in encapsulated form here. Airbnb co founder and CEO Brian Chesky reached out to Nick to ask him to create storyboards because Chesky had just read a biography of Walt Disney. He was inspired by the transition the Walt Disney company made in the 1930s when it shifted from animated shorts to making its first full-length animated motion picture, *Snow White*. The transformation of Disney reminded Chesky of where Airbnb was at the time. The company had just expanded internationally, and Chesky wanted to ensure that everyone in all markets was aligned around the same vision for great host and guest experiences. Thus "Project Snow White" was born.

As Nick recalled, the Airbnb team had worked with internal researchers to identify key moments in the guest and host experiences, ones that were particularly powerful in shaping the nature of the host and guest journey. For example, in the guest journey, one of these moments is when they actually step into the home they've rented for the first time. They have high expectations from the photos they've seen online. Will those promises be fulfilled or will they wish they'd found another place to stay? In the host journey, one important moment is when they return home after the guests have gone. They've entrusted their home to strangers. Have they been respectful, or have they trashed the place?

Cheskey asked Nick Sung to bring all of these moments to life in storyboards to make them vivid, evocative, and emotionally compelling.

In an interview with *Fast Company*, Chesky shared lessons from the process.[1]

> "When you have to storyboard something, the more realistic it is, the more decisions you have to make. Like are these hosts men or women? Are they young, are they old? Where do they live? The city or the countryside? Why are they hosting? Are they nervous? ... [When] they show up to the house, how many bags do they have? How are they feeling? Are they tired? At that point you start designing for stuff for a very particular use case," he continued.

These are the boards for the full host and guest journeys.

Host Journey

Guest Journey

The boards helped the Airbnb team to consider how emotional the experiences of guests and hosts are, encouraging greater empathy for customers. In other words, the boards helped Airbnb mindshift.

Nathan Blecharczyk, co founder of the company, described creating them as "a galvanizing event in the company. We all now know what 'frames' of the customer experience we are working to better serve."[2] Each frame can be thought of as a unique problem space, helping the company to focus on those special moments as they seek ways to enhance customer experiences.

The storyboards were also used to guide decision-making about advertising, marketing, and branding. They are now famous, not only within the company but also in service, marketing, brand, leadership, and culture communities around the world.

For a long time, the boards were displayed in the lobby of Airbnb's headquarters in San Francisco. They were put there to remind employees to always keep the experiences of hosts and guests in mind.

The display read in part as follows:

As you explore Snow White, consider:

- What is the person thinking and feeling in each frame?

- What motivates these characters to progress in their journeys?

- What opportunities exist to improve or enhance the experience for them?

- How does your work influence what the character feels, knows, thinks, decides, or does?

NIKE:
Just Believe It

Storyboarding helps you achieve believability in your story by prodding you to provide sufficient detail about the characters, their hopes and fears, and the challenges they're facing, to make them real to your audience. Just think about the feats of believability Pixar has pulled off: In *Toy Story*, convincing us that our toys might actually be alive. In *Ratatouille*, making us root for a rat in his quest to become a master chef.

Nick shared that also vital to making your story believable is that you first have to believe it yourself. He recalled how when he was working on the movie *Up*, even though he and his team were drawing scenes day in and day out, when they attended the developmental screenings, they would leave crying. The characters and the difficulties they were going through had become real to them.

He emphasized that one key to achieving this believability in creating boards is to draw on your personal experiences, just as Pete Docter did in his conceptualizing of the *Monsters, Inc* story. Whereas for his Airbnb boards, the process started with the data on customer experiences the company had researched, for another storyboarding assignment, Nick emphasized, the starting point was personal experience.

Nike asked him to come in for a workshop to help one of their teams with exploring the emotional journey of people who've been casual athletes and become more dedicated to a sport. One of Nike's missions, as described by founder Phil Knight, has been to be a partner to, and supporter of, athletes who are especially dedicated to their training, really pushing themselves. As he said in one talk, discussing how the company wanted to be there for those runners who go out for their runs no matter how tired they may be or what the weather may be, "When you get up at 5 o'clock in the morning to go for a run, even if it's cold and wet out, you go. And when you get to mile 4, we're the one standing under the lamp post, out there in the cold and wet with you, cheering you on."[3] In that spirit, the team at the workshop hoped to learn more about the journey for those who become so highly devoted to a sport.

The boards Nick drew focused on moments in that journey of becoming that are, as he described, "fraught with hope, uncertainty, challenge and reward." The intent was for the images to allow Nike to have a dialog about what needs, emotions, and actions to design for. As these few boards on the opposite page show, which are a selection of the total set he created, they did so beautifully.

The story told was of a casual runner who decides she's going to run a full marathon. As you look at these boards, consider, what do they convey about her journey?

I don't know about you, but after seeing these boards, I felt inspired to emulate her. I wanted to strap on my running shoes and go for a really tough run in the mountains around Lake Tahoe. Alas, I was stuck on a plane heading to a conference. (Note to self: go on that run!)

For a time, Nick's storyboards were displayed at Nike headquarters in Beaverton, Oregon, to help employees to keep in mind the company's inspirational mission.

I hope they've also inspired you to give storyboarding a try.

Designing Your Storyboard

Don't worry, you don't have to be an artist like Nick. I'm certainly not, and I create storyboards for my work all the time. There are so many generative artificial intelligence (AI) tools out there to help you visualize your story. Your storyboard can also be just a rough sketch, which you craft for your own purposes rather than showing your audience. Simple stick figure drawings will be just fine. Even the artists at Pixar start with rough sketching.

Pixar advises that as you work on your boards, it's a good idea to share them with some trusted others to get their feedback and input, like your personal focus group. These trusted advisors will help you see gaps in your story, or parts that aren't coming through clearly, and make other suggestions that will help you improve it.

> "What happens when I tell the story to another person, is that these other things show up, without me asking for them, even while I'm telling them. The story starts to come alive. The characters start to come alive. And then also the person you told the story to will tell you what they thought of it...They actually are helping you make your story and characters better."[4]

As Pixar advises, we can't possibly account for all the nuances or key points on the first go-round, or even quite possibly, the 29th! It can take Pixar scriptwriters up to 30 attempts to get the story right.

The more you run through the story flow with your trusted early screeners, the more great insights they'll offer. Then you can adapt your story and how you tell it.

Basically, a storyboard is a series of cells, whether they're drawings or photographs, that are physically arranged to tell a story in sequence.[5] If you use presentations such as PowerPoint or Keynote, think of your storyboard as a series of slides. They're designed to illustrate in one sitting all the work you've done in trendsighting, creating your trendscape canvas and considering the elements of powerful stories that you want to incorporate.

Let's use this storyboarding worksheet to get you started, at least with understanding how to outline your story.

STORYBOARD # _____

Step 1:
Define Your Audience

As you define your story, you must tailor it to your audience. Are you creating your story for a senior decision-maker at your company, say in the product design group? Or maybe it's for a group of colleagues or another team? Your audience might also be another kind of stakeholder, like a government official with the authority to support, or nix, the innovation you're championing. The audience might also be the company as a whole.

To define your audience, consider the following:

- What is their name? Make them real.
- What is their role?

Their role will influence what they need to hear from you. For example, if they're the chief financial officer (CFO), they'll likely be particularly concerned about the expense involved and how the initiative will enhance revenues and profitability. A chief operating officer (COO) might, instead, be more focused on practicalities of creating the product or service you're proposing, such as how much new equipment might be needed or what supply chain challenges might be presented. A board member will be keen to hear how the investment community will assess the decision to go ahead with the innovation.

- What's their ambition? What drives them?
- How do they define success?
- What are their weaknesses? Where are they imperfect?
- What keeps them up at night?
- Who are their heroes?
- Who are their villains?
- What are their aspirations, their dreams?
- How do others measure their success?
- What is their happily ever after?

Step 2:
Imagine Your Storyboard as a Story Arc

The best arcs involve increasing dramatic tension, culminating in the climax. As depicted in this figure, seven stages in an arc will generally work well: 1) an opening or exposition, 2) inciting incident, which leads to rising action, 3) which then introduces a crisis, 4) followed by the story climax where everything comes to a head, 5) resulting in success or failure, then 6) the falling action where tension fades and action eases up, and 7) finally, the conclusion brings resolution.[6]

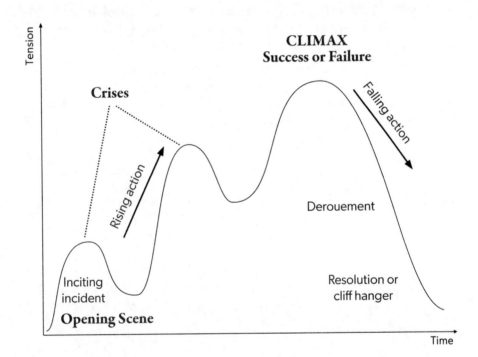

But feel free to use this just as a reference model. The story you tell is yours to define. Build upon this suggested model in any ways that your creativity inspires you to. You may want to embellish this with more elements of the hero's journey, for example.

Indeed, great storytellers have devised many variations on this basic arc. One of them you might consider is to begin your story with its ending. This is a popular movie trope because it grips the audience so powerfully. It was used in the 1950 classic *Sunset Boulevard*, with the opening scene showing the story's protagonist floating dead in a swimming pool, with a voice-over of him reflecting on the nature of the tragedy that unfolded to lead him to that denouement. More recently, the technique was used in the huge hits *Deadpool* and *Ratatouille*.[7]

Starting with the ending can be powerful in mindshifting because it allows you to right away portray the better future you're trying to tell and sell. It's a way of hooking your audience with a compelling vision that motivates them to hear your case for it. You might also grip them by portraying the future they don't want to experience in the store. Maybe that would be a scene of the liquidation of the last remaining stock of a retailer that has succumbed to bankruptcy, which might include a sad image of the store's empty shelves. Your opening might also be to portray both a positive and negative scenario, side by side, or one right after the other, to prompt the question, which future do you want?

Outline the Key Moments in Your Story, the Story Beats

I've drawn on a great set of questions to help with this that were posted by author Venecia Williams to develop this set[8]:

- What is the most important thing for the audience to know and why?
- What is the first impression you want them to have?
- What does the audience need to know first to help them grasp your desired takeaways?
- What would be the second thing they need to know?
- The third?
- The fourth?
- How does this information change their tomorrow?
- What happens to them, what benefits do they gain, if they respond to this trend now?
- What happens if they wait?
- What happens if they do nothing?
- What does success look like on each horizon?

Your answers will help you determine the scenes through which you tell your story. Imagine the outcomes, creatively, based on the evidence collected during the development of your trendscape canvas. Then take some time to consider what you should say or show differently to better grab people's attention and help them see the trend in a way they can understand and internalize.

Step 4:
Define the Goal of Each Cell or Page of Your Storyboard

Craft a purpose or impact statement under each cell. An impact statement demonstrates the meaning of that moment and how it contributes to affecting or impacting the lives of your characters (and your audience).[9] For example, for Nick Sung's storyboard of the marathoner looking out the window of her hotel room, the impact statement might be:

> She's wondering whether she's ready and thinking *I can't believe I'm here.* She asks herself, what if I'm not good enough? We're moved, and she becomes even more relatable.

Each story beat comes to life in your visualization to convey the purpose of that moment for your story. Writing these purpose statements helps you see how all of the beats add up to the grander story you're going to tell. These purpose statements will also be important in writing the verbal script of your story.

That's the next step in your mindshifting journey. But first, one last point to make about storyboarding is that it can be a great practice for working out the future we'd like to create for ourselves in our own lives as well.

We generally go through life without taking the time to carefully craft each chapter of the story we'd love to live. But that can change. Imagine your next year, two years, five years, as a storyboard. How would you tell your story? Where would you be at the end of each milestone? What would life look like along the way, frame by frame?

Some fascinating research in psychology put people through an exercise related to this, which led to life-enhancing effects. As reported by Eric Dolan, the researchers first asked people to write their life story, and then they requested that people rewrite that story so that it followed the narrative arch of the hero's journey.[10] One of the researchers, Benjamin Rogers, explained, "We theorized that life stories aligning with this timeless, universally appealing narrative would be perceived as more meaningful." That's just what they found. By reframing their life stories as closely aligned with the hero's journey, people felt increased well-being and a greater sense of purpose and meaning in their lives. And what's more, they felt more resilient about the challenges they were facing in their lives. "This is particularly relevant today," Rogers shared, "as many sense a prevailing crisis of meaning in contemporary times."

So why not storyboard both your past and your future as your personal Hero's Journey?

Your life is your story to create. Why not make it a great one?

Chapter 12

Achieve

> # "Do not go where the path may lead, go instead where there is no path and leave a trail."
>
> —Ralph Waldo Emerson

No story can change someone's mind unless they want to listen. A big part of your job is to get people to listen.

You do that in part by crafting a great story. But you also do it by thoughtfully considering who your audience is and how best to go about sharing your story with them.

Steve Jobs was so successful as a storyteller not only because of how well he could tell a story but because he understood how to speak to the early adopters who would be most receptive to his vision and would be crucial to igniting the wider mindshifts he championed. His presentations for launching new Apple products have become legendary.

But let's take a look at a much earlier example of his storytelling, in a speech he gave at the International Design Conference in Aspen, Colorado, in June 1983. He was speaking to product designers, and he deeply understood their desire for great design to be a more powerful force in creating products. That was a desire he shared with them, and it's not hard to imagine how powerfully he moved them in this speech.

> One of the reasons I'm here is because I need your help. If you've looked at computers, they look like garbage. All the great product designers are off designing automobiles or buildings. But hardly any of them are designing computers. If we take a look, we're going to sell 3 million computers this year, 10 million in '86, whether they look like a piece of shit or they look great...And it doesn't cost any more money to make them look great. They are going to be these new objects that are going to be in everyone's working environment, everyone's educational environment, and everyone's home environment. We have a shot [at] putting a great object there...
>
> We have a chance to make these things beautiful, and we have a chance to communicate something through the design of the objects themselves.[1]

Where he led, they followed, and the rest, as they say, is history.

Considered to be one of the greatest NFL coaches in history, Vince Lombardi once famously said that

> "A leader is a visionary that energizes others. This definition of leadership has two key dimensions: a) creating the vision of the future, and b) inspiring others to make the vision a reality."[2]

Jobs was a master of both. He created aspirational and moving visions of a better future, and he inspired others to follow his call to action. One reason he was so effective in mobilizing action was that he had a deep understanding of who those who would form the vanguard would be and what they also cared about. There was a shared vision in making the impossible possible.

Focus First on a Significant Minority

In my research about change agents and large-scale change initiatives, I found that most of the executives leading them make the mistake of kicking off a big change campaign by trying to convince everybody at once. They rely largely on efforts to create a widespread sense of urgency, the technique known as describing the current situation as a "burning platform." But no matter how urgent the need for change may be, many people will resist it.

Different groups within an organization will typically have particular reasons for their resistance. For example, executives may resist change because they do not feel aligned or connected to the future being depicted. Or they may not feel motivated or incentivized by financial objectives or compensation.

Managers may resist because they, too, don't feel plugged in, or perhaps they feel like they are losing control over their routines and people or that they're overwhelmed with change on top of everything else in their day-to-day work.

Employees may resist because they don't have insight into the purpose of change and also because they don't feel a sense of ownership of the process. They may also not see what's in it for them.

People in all of these positions may feel like their comfort zone is threatened or fear the unknown, even if they're fully aware of that dread.

In addition, most people these days are feeling change fatigue. In fact, this was true well before the rapid innovation cycles we see today. In 2014, a report by PwC found that 65% of corporate workers cited change fatigue.[3] They complained that they didn't understand the reasons for change or what individual or collective success looked like on the other side. In fact, almost 40% said that they didn't agree with it.

Gartner's research in 2020 produced similar findings. In fact, Gartner analysts found that the propensity for change fatigue doubled during the pandemic of 2020.

A study published by Capterra in 2022 found that change fatigue is making employee burnout worse, at record levels.[4] The workforce is placing the blame on leaders, with 71% of employees saying they're overwhelmed by the amount of change at their job. More so, 83% of workers suffering from change fatigue say their employer has not provided enough tools or resources to help them adapt. And with change becoming constant, leaders must open their minds, or new leaders with open minds must rise, to do more to help employees adapt to change. Seventy-eight percent of employees expect constant change to happen at their job moving forward. Legacy leadership is doing only what it knows how to do. What's painfully clear is that these old ways of "leading" are no longer working. What's more, these leaders cannot recognize that they're part of the problem. This creates a vicious cycle of debilitating leadership.

Prosci, an organization focused on helping organizations change, has written extensively on how this vicious cycle creates resistance. In its research, Prosci identified eight categories of what resistance looks like.

- **Emotion**: Fear, loss, sadness, anger, anxiety, frustration, depression, focus on self

- **Disengagement:** Silence, ignoring communications, indifference, apathy, low morale

- **Work impact:** Reduced productivity/efficiency, noncompliance, absenteeism, mistakes

- **Acting out:** Conflict, arguments, sabotage; overbearing, aggressive or passive-aggressive behavior

- **Negativity:** Rumors/gossip, miscommunication, complaining, focus on problems, celebrating failure

- **Avoidance:** Ignoring the change, reverting to old behaviors, workarounds, abdicating responsibilities

- **Building barriers:** Excuses, counter approaches, recruiting dissenters, secrecy, breakdown in trust

- **Controlling:** Asking lots of questions, influencing outcomes, defending the current state, using status.

To break through the resistance, you will need to work to create alignment with others in the organization and help them overcome their reluctance to change. You can then elicit their support in building momentum for it. You have to be highly strategic about building support first with key people who are likely to be more receptive and who can help you gain leverage.

The key is to find your significant minority. In his renowned book *Diffusion of Innovations*, Everett M. Rogers explained how new ideas and technology spread.[5] His research demonstrated that it takes only 10–20% of the individuals in a population to adopt a new idea or innovation for rapid acceptance by the majority to follow.[6]

Rather than trying to reach everyone or focusing on trying to convince the contrarians or cynics, find the people who are frustrated with the way things are. Find the people who are excited about new opportunities or the people who are anxious or worried about the unknown. Share your story with them, including the role they play in leading change and what's in it for them.

As you consider who these early supporters may be, look for two key types.

Type 1 **Change advocates**	Type 2 **Transformation executives**
These are individuals who are passionate about trends, the art of the possible, and innovations who actively spread the word about their potential to colleagues and executives. They deeply believe that transformation and innovation is necessary to thrive in the long term. Even though they realize they don't have experience in navigating corporate change or guiding change management, they feel like not doing something is not an option. But they still live and operate in the "ordinary world" and have not yet received their "call to adventure." You can be the one to ignite their change energy.	These changemakers are officially tasked with heading transformational efforts in specific business units. They're motivated to listen to ideas for innovations and can provide support of many kinds. That might be providing funding for pilot projects that can provide proof of concept. Or it might be advocating for you in the C-suite or providing you with the opportunity to make your argument to the executive team yourself.

Also make note of those who fall into two other key groups and may make or break your efforts:

- **Linchpins:** These are the executives who are vital to an enterprise. As decision-makers and influencers, they make things happen or block progress.

- **Saboteurs:** They will stand in front of any effort to change their status quo, challenge their authority or status, or threaten their way of working.

You will need to anticipate resistance from them and be highly intentional about how you respond to it.

This will be true even in sharing your vision for change with your significant minority. Many of them will also likely raise concerns or outright objections to the change you're advocating. Don't just tell them your story; also seek their input and listen thoughtfully to their feedback, including any objections. You want to convert them into collaborators, and to do that, you must be collaborative. That means being open-minded and willing to take in alternative perspectives with genuine curiosity and appreciation. Draw on the work you've done to cultivate a beginner's mind and to stay aware of your own biases and how they might cloud your judgment about people's reactions. Get into your growth mindset to be receptive to criticisms of your vision and work with others to hone it, or even to make a pivot to an alternative way forward. Many of the most successful innovations have benefited from critical, even harsh, feedback that unlocked limitations to the concept and opened the door to better solutions.

Peter Senge, author of the business classic *The Fifth Discipline* and a pioneer of organizational learning, observed, "People don't resist change; they resist being changed."[7] Those advocating change are often too insistent about their own views, trying to force others to see things their way. That's counterproductive. People become especially resistant when they feel change is being imposed upon them rather than that they are being included in deciding about the change needed and have a say in how to achieve it. This is another main reason that so many corporate change efforts fail; they've being imposed from the top down.

Not all resistance is negative; sometimes it's quite constructive. Fire up your curiosity, and tune up your receiver's state of mind. You've learned a great deal about the opportunities and threats you've charted, but as you share those insights, you will have so much more to learn.

Begin Socializing Your Story

In the world of organizational change, socializing is the act of telling your story to key colleagues, and ultimately to decision-makers. You want to socialize your story of change in the ways that people communicate in your organization and have historically been prompted into action. I call this using their "love language" to connect the story with them, in their way. You can consult all sorts of company resources to help get up to speed with the preferred language, such as existing decks, reports, videos of town halls, meeting agendas, and corporate communications on the company website.

Your goal is to gain organizational clout and credibility by connecting to people, fostering meaningful relationships, and building an internal network of influence. This necessarily involves establishing new relationships outside of your area of operation.

Change efforts are bigger than any one person or department. They often require cross-functional resources for support and to be properly executed and funded. You must therefore make allies across departments, business units, and key stakeholder groups. This is not always easy. Colleagues can be territorial. They might guard information or processes, claiming ownership over them. When approaching stakeholders, you must be genuine and take any personal agendas off the table to remove any perceived threats to the stakeholder's "territory." You must also understand your colleagues' perspectives, beliefs, and realities, to find common ground with them.

This relationship building may be uncomfortable at first, feeling like you're politicking. I understand. I do not like politics in the workplace at all. But I go all in on relationships. That wasn't always the case, though. Of all the things I've done in my life, cultivating and maintaining strategic relationships has been my weakness. I used to marvel at how some of the most successful people in my life rose to their positions and continued to thrive in life. I always just thought it came down to the work, the time, the focus. But no. I learned it really comes down to networking and relationship building. As an introvert, this is something I'm still learning and practicing.

The good news is that with that practice, the process becomes almost second nature. Remember, your intentions are virtuous. You're leading an effort to unite people around common threats and opportunities. You're fighting the good fight.

As you cultivate these relationships, you can draw on the wisdom of some of the most influential authorities on achieving influence through relationships.

In his influential book *How to Win Friends and Influence People*, Dale Carnegie observed, "[T]he only way on earth to influence other people is to talk about what they want and show them how to get it."[8] Carnegie's approach to influencing people is rooted in building meaningful, productive, mutually beneficial relationships. He advocates the following guidelines:

- Don't criticize, condemn, or complain.
- Give honest and sincere appreciation.
- Become genuinely interested in other people.
- Be a good listener. Encourage others to talk about themselves.
- Talk in terms of the other person's interests.
- Make the other person feel important—and do it sincerely.
- Remember that a person's name is to that person the sweetest and most important sound in any language.
- Let the other person feel that the idea is his or hers.
- Try honestly to see things from the other person's point of view.[9]

It's so important as you reach out to your significant minority to learn what's important to them, what motivates them, and to listen thoughtfully, not dismissing or diminishing their perspectives. You have to keep in mind how different their experiences with the organization may be and how differently they may think and feel about the disruptive possibilities you're describing.

This calls to mind a little demonstration in perspective that my friend, the master storyteller Michael Margolis, taught me. My friend, Robert Tercek, a fellow futurist and co-host of *The Futurists* podcast, was talking with Margolis.

He raised his hand with just his index finger pointing upward and asked, "What is this?" We were afraid to answer as we weren't sure if this was a trick question.

"It's a finger pointing up," I said.

Brett replied, "It's the number 1."

Margolis replied, "You're both right."

"It's also an index finger; it could also mean to hold for a moment or to ask a question."

In European visual art, the finger pointing upwards suggest the existence or presence of God.[10]

Margolis' point is that it could mean different things to different people all dependent on the context.

It's also a reminder that people hear and see things differently. It's helpful in keeping in mind that you must persuade people about your story not from the position of where you are, but from where they are.

While the age-old golden rule says that we must treat others as we want to be treated, when it comes to championing change, especially if you're navigating a culture of hierarchy and politics, you need a twist on the golden rule: treat others as they want to be treated.

More sage advice about cultivating these supportive relationships comes from author and entrepreneur Keith Ferrazzi, whom I've been fortunate to work with. He developed the concept of Relationship Action Planning, which he defines as "the act of proactively working to advance relationships with the people most important in achieving your business plans."[11] He emphasizes that relationships should not be thought of as transactional, but rather as about serving others. "At the core of every relationship is generosity," he writes. "Reaching out to other people to be of service. Generosity builds relationship strength quickly."[12]

In addition to identifying all those who will either be likely supporters or likely, or possible, saboteurs, he advises prioritizing which relationships you want to cultivate, as well as regularly assessing the strength of the relationships formed so that you can most effectively allocate your time to these efforts.[13]

I think I should say something here for anyone who may be skeptical of taking such a strategic approach to relationship building. I get it. After all, there are a lot of people who are disingenuous self-servers out there. But, as long as your purpose is virtuous and inclusive, as long as your intent is just and focused on the betterment of people's lives, as long as that's what really drives you, then the more intentional you are about this process, the better you will be fulfilling that purpose.

Going Wide with Trendfluence

Having gained the support of your significant minority, it's time to spread the word more widely. That might be in a presentation to a group of decision-makers, such as the executive team of your organization, or it might be in a presentation to a larger group of stakeholders, such as potential funders.

No initiative can gain significant, enterprise-wide traction without support from the top. This is when you will strategically tell your full mindshift story, marshaling all of the data you've gathered and the storyline you've developed to engage and excite the linchpin arbiters who can either embrace your vision and greenlight a roadmap for acting on it or shut you down.

As you prepare to tell your story to them, keep in mind that they inhabit a different world within the organization, with many concerns and responsibilities that you're not privy to. They're primarily concerned with the demands of their shareholders, investors, and boards. They speak the language of the C-suite, and you should learn to speak it too. In particular, as you present the trends and vision you've crafted, you must clarify what the value of the change you're advocating is for the organization, ideally in the terms that are familiar to them. What return on their investment can they anticipate? What advantage can they gain over competitors? What new market segments will they appeal to?

Be aware of how removed from the trenches of the disruption you're tracking they may be. They're often also insulated from receiving input from within the ranks. I'm reminded of a story about Cees 't Hart, CEO of the Carlsberg Group, a global brewery and beverage company. On his first day as CEO, 'T Hart was given a special elevator key card by his assistant to go directly to his corner office on the 20th floor with a beautiful view of Copenhagen.[14] After his first two months, he realized, unsurprisingly, that he rarely interacted with other Carlsberg employees. He didn't want to be so removed from them and from the culture of the larger organization. So, he decided to move from his corner office to an empty desk in an open-floor plan on a lower floor.

Executives may also suffer especially badly from the closed-mindedness of the expert's mind. A great deal of research has demonstrated that most leaders are woefully unaware of their shortfalls. In one study, for example, of more than 3,600 leaders, the researchers found that higher-level leaders significantly overvalued their skills compared with how others perceived them.[15] In other words, they don't know what they don't know.

To inspire them to mindshift, you must not only tell a great story but tell it in a way that will surprise, delight, and excite them. In doing so, your delivery will be every bit as important as the story structure and the drama of emotion your story evokes. Here you can draw on the talents of great orators, and there is no better place to start than with the insights of the first specialist on rhetoric.

When I was in elementary school, I loved any class that explored ancient history. I was enamored by stories of ancient Greece and Greek philosophy. There was one lesson I'll never forget. I also remember the hand-drawn cover for the report I submitted on the subject; it was my personal take on Aristotle's "ethos, logos, and pathos." That lesson inspired this shy, introverted kid to enlist in speech club and participate in competitions involving other elementary schools. I wasn't any good then, but I'll never forget the experience.

Logos, ethos, and pathos—this is the recipe that determines how well a storyteller appeals to their audience.

In the 4th century BC, Aristotle studied orators of the day, mainly politicians and lawyers. At the time, public speaking became an essential skill for politicians. Ordinary citizens too, learned to demonstrate oration skills in courts of law. His goal was to understand the elements and techniques that made for a compelling speech. His work became a treatise about how to persuade others of your views. Titled *The Art of Rhetoric*, it is widely regarded as "the most important single work on persuasion ever written."[16]

Aristotle's Rhetorical Triangle

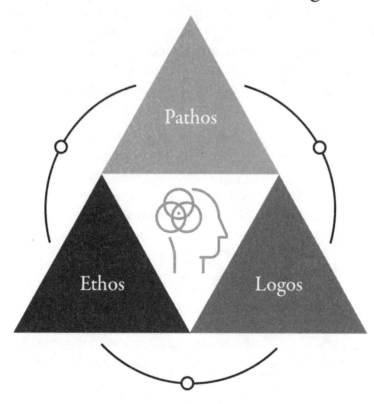

In Aristotle's own words…

> Of the modes of persuasion furnished by the spoken word there are three kinds.
>
> The first kind depends on the personal character of the speaker; [ethos]
>
> the second on putting the audience into a certain frame of mind; [pathos]
>
> the third on the proof, or apparent proof, provided by the words of the speech itself. [logos]
>
> Persuasion is achieved by the speaker's personal character when the speech is so spoken as to make us think him credible. We believe good men more fully and more readily than others: this is true generally whatever the question is, and absolutely true where exact certainty is impossible and opinions are divided. …
>
> Secondly, persuasion may come through the hearers, when the speech stirs their emotions. Our judgements when we are pleased and friendly are not the same as when we are pained and hostile. …
>
> Thirdly, persuasion is effected through the speech itself when we have proved a truth or an apparent truth by means of the persuasive arguments suitable to the case in question.

Regarding ethos, your delivery style is the foundation for conveying your character. It is as important as the message (logos).

You can make the appeal of ethos more powerful by doing the following:

- Painting a vivid picture that immerses your audience
- Speaking the language of your audience
- Speaking with conviction and confidence (you deserve to stand in front of this audience)
- Not using corporate buzzwords or jargon (unless that is what will resonate)

To make the appeal of your logos more powerful, do the following:

- Use rousing quotes, facts, statistics, endorsements, from people and institutions your audience respects and admires.[17]
- Reference startling research in support of your story that appeals to the audience's intellect.
- Be specific. Don't speak in generalizations.
- Use examples that people can relate to and/or help them understand examples that might seem unrelated at first.

To make the appeal of pathos more powerful, do the following:

- Put a "face" on the problem and opportunity you're exploring.[18]
- Use humor to make your story disarming and relatable. My friends Jennifer Aaker and Naomi Bandanas are the co-authors of the popular book *Humor Seriously: Why Humor is a Secret Weapon in Business and Life*.[19] They surface a major misconception that leaders need to be serious to be taken seriously.[20] Research, however, finds that humor builds bonds, defuses tension, boosts innovation, and bolsters resilience.[21]
- Use language and imagery that plays heart strings beautifully (and delicately).
- Change your tone and pace to stir emotion at key moments, to get someone excited, warmed, emotionally charged, inspired, impassioned, and moved.[22]

Another great orator you can learn from practiced his craft in more recent times. Former President of the United States Barack Obama gave speeches that galvanized people around the world to hope for and build toward a brighter future.

Many experts credit his "oratorical fluency and fervor" for lifting him past more established and known rivals to win the Democratic nomination. He then followed a similar path to win the White House.[23]

Writing for the *Guardian*, British Prime Minister David Cameron described Obama's rhetorical power this way:

> I remember watching with wonderment a video of the "fired up, ready to go" speech he gave on the eve of voting, seeking inspiration as I wrestled with words during my own foray into political speechwriting. It is an astonishing performance, a witty exhortation forged by Obama's heritage, infused with passion and poetry and delivered with immense flair.[24]

Obama is the first Democratic president since Franklin D. Roosevelt to win more than 50% of the popular vote in a re-election run.[25] He is also the only Democratic candidate for president since FDR to twice win more than 50% of the national vote.[26]

In an analysis of Obama's rhetoric, Mylena Origgi, an international executive speaker coach, identified three elements to his mastery.

- Obama contrasted a problem and a solution and communicated how to connect the two to establish authority.
- Obama embraced repetition to make important messages and ideas more memorable and relatable.
- Obama controlled his pace, volume, and timbre for dramatic effect, to engage emotions and captivate attention, which then incited reactions from the crowd, conveyed significance, and catalyzed action.[27]

As you prepare to tell your story to the wider population of those you want to join you in your mindshift, there are innumerable other great sources you can draw on for honing your delivery. For here, I want to leave you with one last piece of advice.

Make the Most of Your Ignite Moment

The moment we first have someone's attention is special. It's a gift. I call it the "ignite moment." It's the moment when we have the invitation and the space from someone to share. You should think creatively about how you can optimize the effect of this moment in sharing your mindshift story.

Ask yourself, what do you want your audience to feel? How can you really grab them? How can you make your ignite moment a powerful call to adventure? How can you get your audience in a receptive, even excited, mindset?

Perhaps you can take some inspiration from one of the most effective ignite moments I've experienced in the many years that I've been studying powerful rhetoric.

When Mohammed Qahtani took the stage at the 2015 World Championship of Public Speaking, he pulled out a cigarette and attempted to light it. That's the exact moment he won over the crowd. They just didn't know it yet.

It's here when the crowd started to react, jeering, rustling in their seats, "No, no, no!"

He looked up, raised his arms before he could light the cigarette, and replied with surprise, "What?"

Everyone started laughing, probably out of surprise and also relief. He then responded by challenging the audience. "Oh, you all think smoking kills?" he asked. "Let me tell you something."

Next came another question. "Do you know that the number of people dying from diabetes is three times as many as people dying from smoking?" he asserted. "Yet, if I pulled out a Snicker bar, nobody would say anything."

Again, the audience laughed along, unsure of where this was all going. Qahtani then argued, "Did you know the leading cause of lung cancer is not actually a cigarette? It's your DNA. You could smoke for years, and nothing would ever happen to you."

The crowd dwelled in silence. At this point, the audience was not sure how to respond. He was incredibly persuasive. People were probably questioning their own knowledge at this point.

"I use these arguments," he said, "...even though I just made them up."

The crowd erupted into laughter.

He then told the story of how he tested this argument with a group of friends. "Two started smoking," he joked.

Qahtani took a serious tone at this point. "Words, when said and articulated in the right way, can change someone's mind."[3]

With that, he had set the stage for a moving talk about the power of words. Our words, and the manner in which we deliver them, really can change the world. Crafting a powerful mindshift story, and delivering it with great ethos, logos, and pathos, is the art and heart of the possible. It's the heart of defining the future we wish to live in. It's at the heart of catalyzing a collective mindshift.

Achievement Requires Resolve

No matter how powerful a story you craft, however, and how inspirational you are in delivering it, you will meet some resistance. That will be true even of some of those you would most expect to immediately appreciate your vision. This is why you must act with resolve.

As Apple's former chief design officer and co founder of LoveFrom, a small collective of creators, Jony Ive is an obsessive student of design and the creative process. In a lecture at

Cambridge University, when receiving the Stephen Hawking Fellowship award, he commended the importance of resolve as the necessary partner to creativity. "There is a fundamental conflict between two very different ways of thinking," Ive observed. "It is the conflict between curiosity and the resolve and focus that is necessary to solve problems."[29]

Yet, he proceeded to emphasize, curiosity and resolve are not truly mutually exclusive. You have to find the balance of dancing between them. While you must be "utterly driven and completely focused to solve apparently insurmountable problems," he continued, "solving those problems requires new ideas." There is a back and forth between exercising your curiosity to keep discovering better ways to solve the problem and digging in to create the solution. "The difference between an idea and a product is that you've solved the problems," Ive observed.

One of my favorite stories of how this dance between curiosity and resolve led to brilliant problem-solving, and a breakthrough achievement, is that of the creation of the iPhone.

Contrary to popular myth, the iPhone was not the brainchild of Steve Jobs. In fact, Jobs almost prevented its creation. Hard to believe, right? Remember, even the disrupters can be disrupted—and can need others to help them prevent being disrupted.

In his book *The One Device: The Secret History of the iPhone*, author Brian Merchant tells the behind-the-scenes story of how the iPhone came into being. At the start, Jobs knew nothing about it. "The iPhone began as an experimental project undertaken without his knowledge," Merchant said in an interview.[30]

The year was 2004, and smartphones were on the rise. Beyond email, what caught the attention of a group of Apple designers was the increasing functionality of phones as cameras and MP3 players. Phones like the Nokia 5310 were becoming more and more popular for their music playing capabilities.[31]

At the time, the iPod accounted for greater than half of Apple's sales.[32] Losing market share to Nokia, or any emergent devices, was not an option. Tony Fadel, the designer of the iPod, who would later go on to develop the first three versions of the iPhone, had a finely tuned receiver's mind.[33] He saw the writing on the wall: Apple needed to invent a phone. "We had the music player doing video and audio and photo," Fadel recounted.[34] "We had iTunes. Then futurephones came out. They started playing MP3. This is a holy shit moment. Phones could steal everything we were doing. What could we do to counter this?"

Apple had proven its creativity in solving existential problems in spades. But the issue this time was that Jobs was no fan of Apple designing a phone. As Merchant recounts, "'The problem with a phone,' Jobs said, 'is that we're not very good going through orifices to get to the end users.' By orifices, he meant carriers like Verizon and AT&T, which had final say over which phones could access their networks."[35]

Jobs also wasn't convinced that the emergent smartphone category would reach a wide-enough market. He believed the potential for smartphones was limited to "pocket protector" or email-obsessed business users.

My friend and early iPhone engineer Andy Grignon shared with Merchant that "The exec team was trying to convince Steve that building a phone was a great idea," but "He didn't really see the path to success."[36] He did decide, though, to contract with phone maker Motorola to make a phone for Apple. This doesn't sound like the Steve Jobs we know, allowing another company to deliver an experience connected to an Apple platform without controlling the user experience. But that's exactly what happened. Jobs hated the final product. But nonetheless, he agreed to go ahead and launch the phone, and it hit the market in September 2005 at the same time as the Moto ROKR E1. It was a total bomb.

Meanwhile, back on November 7, 2004, then Apple Vice President Michael Bell reportedly sent a late-night email to Jobs detailing the reasons that Apple should design its own phone. As the story goes, Jobs called Bell immediately, with the pair debating for hours. Jobs finally relented. But he wanted complete control of the design, without any service providers stepping in. He was so adamant about this that he considered buying cellular spectrum to exclusively sell the phone directly. Apple almost became a mobile virtual network operator! However, Cingular, now AT&T, offered free reign over the design in exchange for exclusivity.

Jobs made another make-or-break demand. He told the team he needed to see an interface that might be intuitive and exciting to lay-users [everyday users], "not just tech product geeks," Merchant reports.

The original iPhone design was anything but. The team made the common mistake of sticking closely to a prior successful design rather than creating a novel solution. They tried to create a phone that was a souped-up version of the company's ultra-successful iPods.

David Tupman, who headed iPod hardware at the time, shared with Merchant. "We put a radio inside, effectively an iPod Mini with a speaker and headphones, still using the touch-wheel interface," he said. It's again hard to believe, but Jobs was a fan of this early design. Others working on the design, however, felt very differently. Grignon revealed, "It was just obvious that we were overloading the click wheel with too much. And texting and phone numbers —it was a f***ing mess."[37]

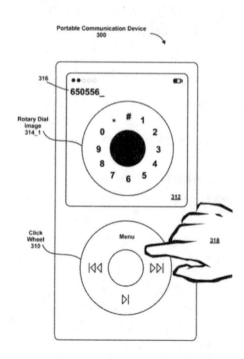

But the team showed great resolve. Though they had won Jobs over, they had a ways to go yet on their hero's journey. They had to dig deeply into their creativity and generate a truly bold new design, which was also beautiful.

"We tried everything," Fadell recalled.[38] "We tried for seven or eight months to get that thing to work. Couldn't do it. We added more buttons and it just became this gangly thing." Finally, they broke free from their resolve to make that design work and reignited their curiosity—what might an entirely different approach to designing a smartphone look like? They danced an exquisite dance from then on, envisioning the beautiful object that made the iPhone so irresistible while also applying their resolve to find solutions to a host of daunting engineering problems. The iPhone was launched in 2007, by Jobs with his awe-inspiring storytelling panache, to thunderous applause.

Grignon would become the first person to receive a call from an iPhone.

As for Fadell, he would found a company called Nest Labs in 2010, with Matt Rogers, where he created the also beautifully enticing Nest Thermostat and proceeded to sell the company to Google in 2014 for $3.2 billion.

The creation of the iPhone is a quintessential story of the power of a mindshift. The design team were open to receiving the signals of emergent disruption. They then astutely perceived that they could combine the brilliance of Apple design with the emergent smartphone trend. Next they wove together their insights about the emerging trend to conceive a powerful story that allowed Jobs to experience his own mindshift. They then together achieved the creation of one of the most successful and influential new products in history no one else saw coming.

Conclusion

If Not You, Who?

In 2011, Denzel Washington delivered a provocative commencement speech for 5,000 graduates of the University of Pennsylvania. He also received an honorary doctorate degree from the Ivy League institution on that day.[1]

The Oscar-winning actor encouraged students not to settle for the status quo but to take risks and embrace failure. "I've found that nothing in life is worthwhile unless you take risks. Nothing," he stated.

He challenged our notion of failure, associating it with taking chances, trying new things, and expanding our own horizons. Do you have the guts to fail?" he asked, not as a question but as a provocation. "If you don't fail, you're not even trying."

Are you taking risks that:

Improve or fix something?

Help someone?

Teach us to grow?

Challenge our conventions?

Make us better?

Think about all the ideas you've had or the observations you've made or the changes you could have made before now, if you just believed in yourself. Now think about them the way Washington encouraged those graduates to consider them.

> Imagine you're on your deathbed—and standing around your bed are the ghosts representing your unfilled potential. The ghosts of the ideas you never acted on. The ghosts of the talents you didn't use. And they're standing around your bed. Angry. Disappointed. Upset. 'We came to you because you could have brought us to life,' they say. 'And now we go to the grave together.' So, I ask you today: How many ghosts are going to be around your bed when your time comes?"

He didn't leave them on a down note, though. He closed with this:

> The world needs your talents.[2]

We all have observations about emerging opportunities and threats. We all have ideas for ways to harness the possibilities to create great new solutions and make life better. We all have hopes and dreams about how we could play a part in changing the world for the better. It may sound like a cliché, but the essential difference between those who change the world and those who get stuck in denial or fear or complacency is that the changemakers take the first step, and then the next, and continue to forge ahead.

Professor Leon C. Megginson once famously observed (although this quote is often misattributed to Charles Darwin), "It is not the strongest of the species that survives, nor the most intelligent…. It is the one that is the most adaptable to change."[3]

At any moment, disruption can strike. Why wait for an uh-oh moment when you can potentially minimize disruption's effects and, better yet, capitalize on it to propel our lives forward?

The best-selling author of some of the world's most unforgettable children's stories, including *Matilda* and *Charlie and the Chocolate Factory*, Roald Dahl, observed, "Somewhere inside all of us is the power to change the world."[4] We just have to believe we are that leader. Recall that the changemakers I studied didn't initially see themselves as leaders of change. They had to convince themselves that they were worthy of leadership and that they had permission to rise up and help others achieve something greater together.

I hope the mindshift journey we've been on together has convinced you that you are that leader.

Remember, your destiny isn't a matter of chance; it's a matter of choice. You have what it takes to be the hero you need and that we all need. Your heart and intuition already know who you can truly become. Stoke your passion. Embrace courage.

This is your mindshift moment. This is also their mindshift moment.

Your future starts now.

Endnotes

Introduction: Mindshift Your Ctrl+Alt+Delete Opportunity

1   Chris Dessi, "Shawn Achor Shares 5 Things You Need to Be Happy (According to His Research)," Inc., October 31, 2016.

2   Anaïs Nin, Seduction of the Minotaur (Chicago, The Swallow Press), p.124.

3   Frieda Fordham, et al, Britannica, Carl Jung entry, accessed January 22, 2024, https://www.britannica.com/biography/Carl-Jung

4   Peter Burns, "7 Viktor Frankl Quotes to Motivate You to Find Your Purpose," Medium, April 7, 2020, https://medium.com/mind-cafe/7-viktor-frankl-quotes-to-motivate-you-to-find-your-purpose-2ece0c64f1d8

5   Weir, Peter, director 1989, Dead Poets Society, Touchstone Pictures, Silver Screen Partners IV.

6   Greg Evans, "This piece of advice from David Bowie remains more relevant than ever," Indy100, May 21, 2020, https://www.indy100.com/showbiz/david-bowie-creative-advice-video-9527031

7   Natalie Labir, quoted on the Fuel Running website, Runner Things #759, June 20,2012, https://www.fuelrunning.com/posts.php?blogFolder=quotes&postYear=2012&postMonth=06&postDay=20&postName=i-am-afraid-yet-fearless-for-fearlessness-is-not-the-absence-of-fear-but-the-bravery-to-do-it-anyway

8   Quote Investigator website, February 3, 2015, https://quoteinvestigator.com/2015/02/03/you-can/

Chapter 1: Executives Don't Know What They Don't Know

1   Alvin Toffler, *Future Shock* (New York: Bantam Books), 1984.

2   Collins dictionary online, https://www.collinsdictionary.com/us/dictionary/english/future-shock

3   Jeffry Bartash, "The Great Renegotiation: Millions of employees quit old jobs for better ones," Marketwatch, April 7, 2022, https://www.marketwatch.com/story/the-great-resignation-pfff-call-it-the-great-rehiring-or-great-job-hop-instead-11649261180/

4   U.S. Bureau of Labor Statistics website, accessed February 8, 2024, https://www.bls.gov/news.release/jolts.t04.htm

5   U.S. Bureau of Labor Statistics website, Job Openings and Labor Turnover Survey, accessed February 8, 2022, https://www.bls.gov/jlt/

6   Greg Daugherty, "What Is Quiet Quitting—and Is It a Real Trend?" Investopedia, December 19, 2023. https://investopedia.com/what-is-quiet-quitting-6743910/

7   Anthony C. Klotz and Mark C. Bolino, "When Quiet Quitting Is Worse Than the Real Thing," Harvard Business Review, September 15, 2022, https://hbr.org/2022/09/when-quiet-quitting-is-worse-than-the-real-thing

8   Tuff Shed website,"Increased Demand for its Products Has Company Hiring Across the Country," June 4, 2020, https://www.tuffshed.com/tuff-shed-adjusts-to-new-economic-factors/

9   Peter Michaelson, "Cynicism: The Battle Cry of the Wimp," WhyWeSuffer.com, August 22, 2012, https://whywesuffer.com/cynicism-the-battle-cry-of-the-wimp/

10 Paul Rogat Loeb, Soul of a Citizen (New York: St. Martins Griffin), 2010 edition, p. 93.

11 David Phelan, "How ChatGPT Suddenly Became Google's Code Red, Prompting Return Of Page And Brin," Forbes, January 23, 2023, https://forbes.com/sites/davidphelan/2023/01/23/how-chatgpt-suddenly-became-googles-code-red-prompting-return-of-page-and-brin/

12 Danny Goodwin, "Survey: 51% of Gen Z women prefer TikTok, not Google, for search," Search Engine Land, September 7, 2023, https://searchengineland.com/gen-z-tiktok-google-search-survey-431345/

13 Prabhakar Raghavan, "Brainstorm Tech 2022: Organizing The World's Information," interview by Brian O'Keefe, Fortune, July 18, 2022, https://fortune.com/videos/watch/Brainstorm-Tech-2022-Organizing-The-Worlds-Information/934585a6-7fb6-41a5-8ef3-e497f8ca2986/

14 Rocky Rotella, "GM's Infamous Racing Ban of 1963," September 14, 2018, pontiacv8.com/blog/2018/9/14/gms-infamous-racing-ban-of-1963/

15 Ibid.

16 Henry Payne, "The real story behind 'Ford v Ferrari'," The Detroit News, November 14, 2019, https://www.detroitnews.com/story/opinion/columnists/henry-payne/2019/11/14/real-story-behind-ford-v-ferrari/2567859001/

17 Chuck Tannert, "Ford vs. Ferrari: The Real Story Behind The Most Bitter Rivalry In Auto Racing," ForbesWheels, November 14, 2019, https://www.forbes.com/wheels/news/ford-vs-ferrari-the-real-story-behind-the-most-bitter-rivalry-in-auto-racing/

18 A.J. Baime, "A War of Speed," Mohawk Blog, September 13, 2017, https://mohawkconnects.com/article/mohawk-blog/war-speed/

19 Wikipedia, List of 24 Hours of Le Mans winners, https://en.wikipedia.org/wiki/List_of_24_Hours_of_Le_Mans_winners/

20 The Story Behind Ford Vs. Ferrari, Volo Auto Sales website, August 26, 2022, https://www.volocars.com/auto-sales/news/ford-vs-ferrari/

21 Erik Bjornstad,"The Real Racing Story of Ford Vs. Ferrarri," Bell Performance website, February 14, 2020, https://www.bellperformance.com/blog/the-real-racing-story-of-ford-v-ferrari/

22 Matthew Phelan, "What's Fact and What's Fiction in Ford v. Ferrari," Slate, November 18, 2019, https://slate.com/culture/2019/11/ford-v-ferrari-fact-vs-fiction-le-mans-ken-miles.html

23 Jason Barlow, "Here's the Real Story Behind the Le Mans-Winning Ford GT40," BBC TopGear website, August 17, 2017, topgear.com/car-news/pioneers/heres-the-real-story-behind-le-mans-winning-ford-gt40-roy-lunn/

24 John Lamm, "The Exhilarating History of Ford's GT40," Revs Institute website, https://www.collierautomedia.com/the-exhilarating-history-of-fords-gt40/

25 Ronnie Schreiber, "How Lee Iacocca and Carroll Shelby changed Detroit," Hagerty website, July 12, 2019, https://www.hagerty.com/media/automotive-history/how-lee-iacocca-and-carroll-shelby-changed-detroit/

26 Michael Wayland, "What to know about Ford's incoming CEO Jim Farley," CNBC website, August 4, 2020, https://www.cnbc.com/2020/08/04/what-to-know-about-fords-incoming-ceo-jim-farley.html

27 Michael Wayland, "Ford's stock is up 70% since Jim Farley became CEO – but he still has a ton of work to do," CNBC website, September 30, 2022, https://www.cnbc.com/2022/09/30/ford-stock-up-70percent-since-jim-farley-became-ceo.html

28 Jason Kincaid, "Tesla Motors Unveils Jaw-Dropping Menlo Park Showroom, TechCrunch, July 19, 2008, https://techcrunch.com/2008/07/19/tesla-motors-unveils-jaw-dropping-menlo-park-showroom/

29 Eric Reed, "How to Buy a Tesla," SmartAsset website, May 8, 2023, https://smartasset.com/investing/how-to-buy-a-tesla/

30 Rob Stumpf, "Tesla's Found a Way Around Direct Sales Bans By Putting Dealerships on Tribal Lands," TheDrive website, November 8, 2022, https://www.thedrive.com/news/teslas-found-a-way-around-direct-sales-bans-by-putting-dealerships-on-tribal-lands/

31 Brett Foote, "Ford CEO Farley Says Marketing Will Focus on Post-Purchase Experience," Ford Authority website, August 15, 2022, https://fordauthority.com/2022/08/ford-ceo-farley-says-marketing-will-focus-on-post-purchase-experience/

32 Ibid.

33 Michael Wayland, "Ford CEO says 65% of U.S. dealers agree to sell EVs under company's investment programs," CNBC website, December 5, 2022, https://www.cnbc.com/2022/12/05/ford-ceo-says-most-us-dealers-agree-to-sell-evs.html

34 Minda Zetlin, "Ford Just Made a Stunning Announcement. Here's What It Means for Customers," Inc., September 17, 2022, https://www.inc.com/minda-zetlin/ford-just-made-a-stunning-announcement-heres-what-it-means-for-customers.html

35 Tom Moloughney, "65% Of Ford Dealers Agree To Ford's Tough EV Selling Terms," Inside EVs website, December 6, 2022, https://insideevs.com/news/610114/ford-modele-dealership-rules/

36 Michael Martinez, "Dealers Push Back on Ford EV Mandates," Automotive News, November 4, 2022, https://www.autonews.com/dealers/ford-dealers-push-back-ev-mandates/

37 Friedrich Nietzsche, Untimely Meditations (Cambridge, England, Cambridge University Press), 1997, p 112.

Chapter 2: You Are The Leader Who's Needed

1   Jony Ive, "The Creative Process Is Fabulously Unpredictable," interview by Rick Tetzeli, posted by Tracy Francis, McKinsey Digital, June 6, 2023, https://www.mckinsey.com/capabilities/mckinsey-digital/our-insights/the-creative-process-is-fabulously-unpredictable-a-great-idea-cannot-be-predicted/

2   "Leadership is about making others feel safe: Simon Sinek at TED 2014," TED blog, Posted by: Kate Torgovnick May, March 21, 2014, https://blog.ted.com/leadership-is-about-making-others-feel-safe-simon-sinek-at-ted2014/

3   Marcel Schwantes, "A Young Steve Jobs Once Gave This Priceless Leadership Lesson. Here It Is in a Few Sentences." Inc., March 28, 2018, https://www.inc.com/marcel-schwantes/a-young-steve-jobs-once-gave-this-priceless-leadership-lesson-here-it-is-in-a-few-sentences.html

4   Interview 1990, All About Steve Jobs.com, interviewer not named, https://allaboutstevejobs.com/videos/misc/future_of_pc_1990/

5   "What Steve Jobs Said When I Asked Him For Entrepreneurial Advice," Rob Kelly, posted on OnGig website, December 10, 2011, https://blog.ongig.com/entrepreneurship/steve-jobs-advice/

6   Carmine Gallo, "As Steve Jobs Once Said, 'People With Passion Can Change The World," Entrepreneur, July 8, 2015, https://www.entrepreneur.com/leadership/as-steve-jobs-once-said-people-with-passion-can-change/248079/

7   "How to Argue and Win Every Time Quotes," Goodreads, https://www.goodreads.com/work/quotes/880590-how-to-argue-win-every-time-at-home-at-work-in-court-everywhere-e

8   Steven Pressfield, "Resistance Thrives in Darkness," Steven Pressfield website, https://stevenpressfield.com/2019/11/resistance-thrives-in-darkness/

9   Steven Pressfield > Quotes > Quotable Quote, Goodreads, https://www.goodreads.com/quotes/596320-fear-is-good-like-self-doubt-fear-is-an-indicator-fear

10 Sir Ken Robinson, "Do schools kill creativity?" TED Talk, February 2006, https://www.ted.com/talks/sir_ken_robinson_do_schools_kill_creativity

11 Clinton Nguyen, "7 world-changing inventions that were ridiculed when they came out," Business Insider, August 2, 2016, https://www.insider.com/inventions-that-were-ridiculed-2016-8

12 Jason Del Rey, "The making of Amazon Prime, the internet's most successful and devastating membership program," Vox, May 3, 2019, https://www.vox.com/recode/2019/5/3/18511544/amazon-prime-oral-history-jeff-bezos-one-day-shipping

13 Interview video with Jeff Bezos, posted on X by Brian Ji, January 5, 2024, https://twitter.com/BrianJji/status/1743482590529573121

14 Stephen R. Covey, The Leader in Me (New York: Simon & Schuster), 2008, p 39.

15 Rahul Goutan Hoom, "Say, You Haven't Done It Yet": Rick Rubin, Known for Changing Musicians' Lives, Got Saved From Personal Demons Through Surfing Icon's Golden Advise," Essentially Sports, December 24, 2022, https://www.essentiallysports.com/us-sports-news-olympics-news-surfing-news-say-you-havent-done-it-yet-rick-rubin-known-for-changing-musicians-lives-got-saved-from-personal-demons-through-surfing-icons-golden-advise/

Chapter 3: A Self-Aware Mind Is a Shiftable Mind: Get to Know Your Mind

1 Kendra Cherry, "What Is Self-Awareness?," VeryWellMind website, March 10, 2023, https://verywellmind.com/what-is-self-awareness-2795023/

2 Tasha Eurich, "What Self-Awareness Really Is (and How to Cultivate It)," Harvard Business Review, January 4, 2018, https://hbr.org/2018/01/what-self-awareness-really-is-and-how-to-cultivate-it/

3 Ibid.

4 Sala, Fabio. (2003). Executive Blind Spots: Discrepancies Between Self- and Other-Ratings. Consulting Psychology Journal: Practice and Research. 55. 222-229. 10.1037/1061-4087.55.4.222. https://www.researchgate.net/publication/232559373_Executive_Blind_Spots_Discrepancies_Between_Self-_and_Other-Ratings/

5 Elizabeth Perry, "What is self-awareness and how to develop it," BetterUp website, September 14, 2022, https://betterup.com/blog/what-is-self-awareness/

6 Ibid Eurich.

7 Ibid.

8 Jennifer Pittman "Speaking Truth to Power: The Role of the Executive," Markkula Center for Applied Ethics website, February 1, 2007, https://www.scu.edu/ethics/focus-areas/business-ethics/resources/speaking-truth-to-power-the-role-of-the-executive/

9 Joseph Folkman, "Top Ranked Leaders Know This Secret: Ask For Feedback," Forbes, January 8, 2015, https://www.forbes.com/sites/joefolkman/2015/01/08/top-ranked-leaders-know-this-secret-ask-for-feedback/?sh=1448397d3195/

10 "19 unconscious biases to overcome and help promote inclusivity," Asana website, October 9, 2022, https://asana.com/resources/unconscious-bias-examples/

11 Alex Larralde "Unconscious Bias Examples and How to Overcome Them," BetterWorks website, July 21, 2023 https://betterworks.com/magazine/unconscious-bias-examples-and-how-to-overcome-them/

12 "Why am I always so negative?" Dr. Rick Hanson website, https://rickhanson.com/topics-for-personal-growth/the-negativity-bias/

13 Ibid Larralde.

14 "Workplace negativity can hurt productivity," MSUTodaywebsite, February 25, 2015, https://msutoday.msu.edu/news/2015/workplace-negativity-can-hurt-productivity/

15 Tim Fitzpatrick "Effective Ways on How to Shift a Negative Mindset Into Positive," Rialto Marketing website, https://rialtomarketing.com/shift-negative-mindset/

16 Michelle Amerman, "How Negativity Sabotages Your Success," Pathways website, https://pathwaysreallife.com/negativity-sabotages-success/

17 Richard J. Davidson, Panel: The Affect of Emotions: Laying the Groundwork in Childhood, "Understanding Positive and Negative Emotion," Project on the Decade of the Brain, Library of Congress; https://loc.gov/loc/brain/emotion/Davidson.html; also

18 "7 powerful ways to overcome the victim mindset," 7 Mindsets website, https://7mindsets.com/overcome-victim-mindset/

19 Karen Hertzberg, "5 Simple Ways to Write About Negative Issues With a Positive Spin," Grammarly website, May 7, 2019, https://www.grammarly.com/blog/5-simple-ways-write-negative-issues-positive-spin/

20 19 unconscious biases, Asana.

21 "Six Cognitive Biases That Affect Your Leadership," Australia Institute of Business website, July 21, 2021, https://www.aib.edu.au/blog/leadership/six-cognitive-biases-that-affect-your-leadership/

Chapter 4: The Beginner's Mind

1 La Marcel Proust, *In Search of Lost Time*, Volume 5, La Prisonnière (New York: Modern Library), 1993.

2 Amy Tikkanen Timeline of the Titanic's Final Hours," Britannica website, https://www.britannica.com/story/timeline-of-the-titanics-final-hours#:~:text=After%20receiving%20iceberg%20warnings%20throughout,ship's%20speed%20is%20not%20lowered.

3 Amy Tikkanen, "Thomas Andrews," Britannica website, https://www.britannica.com/biography/Thomas-Andrews-Irish-ship-designer/

4 James Camerson, Titanic screenplay, accessed at: https://www.dailyscript.com/scripts/Titanic.txt

5 Kaplan, J., Gimbel, S. & Harris, S. Neural correlates of maintaining one's political beliefs in the face of counterevidence. Sci Rep 6, 39589 (2016). https://doi.org/10.1038/srep39589/

6 "Here's Why People Become Angry When Their Political Beliefs Are Challenged," CBS News website, February 15, 2017, https://www.cbsnews.com/losangeles/news/heres-why-people-become-angry-when-their-political-beliefs-are-challenged/

7 Ibid.

8 "50 Brands that Failed to Innovate," Valuer website, July 28, 2022, https://www.valuer.ai/blog/50-examples-of-corporations-that-failed-to-innovate-and-missed-their-chance/

9 Tenelle Porter & Karina Schumann (2018) Intellectual humility and openness to the opposing view, Self and Identity, 17:2, 139-162, DOI: 10.1080/15298868.2017.1361861, https://www.tandfonline.com/doi/full/10.1080/15298868.2017.1361861/

10 Dr. Daoshing Ni, "The Frog at the Bottom of the Well," Tao of Wellness website, January 2022, https://www.taoofwellness.com/newsletters-blog/2022/2/1/the-frog-at-the-bottom-of-the-well/

11 Ibid.

12 Christian Jarrett "How to foster 'shoshin'," Psyche website, https://psyche.co/guides/how-to-cultivate-shoshin-or-a-beginners-mind/

13 "The Story of a Simple Cup of Tea," GloveWorx website, March 16, 2017, https://www.gloveworx.com/blog/simple-cup-of-tea-story/

14 Ibid.

15 Emma Newlyn, "The benefits of a beginner's mind," EkhartYoga website, https://ekhartyoga.com/articles/practice/the-benefits-of-a-beginners-mind/

16 Fuyu, "Who is Shunryu Suzuki?" https://www.zen-buddhism.net/famous-zen-masters/shunryu-suzuki.html

17 Tom Butler-Bowden, "Zen Mind, Beginner's Mind" on Tom Butler-Bowden website, http://www.butler-bowdon.com/shunryu-suzuki---zen-mind-beginners-mind.html

18 Tom Butler-Bowdon, 50 Spiritual Classics: Timeless Wisdom from 50 Great Books of Inner Discovery, Enlightenment & Purpose. (Londog: Nicholas Brealey Publishing), 2005, pp. 244–245.

19 Ibid Butler-Bowen Zen Mind

20 Ibid.

21 David Chadwick, review of Zen Mind, Beginner's Mind, by Shunryu Suzuki, Inquiring Mind website, Fall 2008, Vol. 25, #1,inquiringmind.com/article/2501_31_chadwick/

22 Marie-Dominique Chenu "St. Thomas Aquinas," Marie-Dominique Chenu Britannica website, accessed January 24, 2024, https://britannica.com/biography/Saint-Thomas-Aquinas/

23 Shunryu Suzuki, Zen Mind, Beginner's Mind, 40th Anniversary Edition (Boston: Shambhala Books), 2010, p 16.

24 Andrea Mathews, "The Closed Mind," Psychology Today website, July 6, 2019, https://www.psychologytoday.com/us/blog/traversing-the-inner-terrain/201907/the-closed-mind/

25 Jarrett, How to foster

26 Colucci-D'Amato L, Bonavita V, di Porzio U. The end of the central dogma of neurobiology: stem cells and neurogenesis in adult CNS. Neurol Sci. 2006 Sep;27(4):266-70. doi: 10.1007/s10072-006-0682-z. PMID: 16998731., https://pubmed.ncbi.nlm.nih.gov/16998731/

27 Maglić M, Pavlović T and Franc R (2021) Analytic Thinking and Political Orientation in the Corona Crisis. Front. Psychol. 12:631800. doi: 10.3389/fpsyg.2021.631800, https://www.frontiersin.org/articles/10.3389/fpsyg.2021.631800/full/; see also, Eric W. Dolan, "Large study finds closed-mindedness predicts non-compliance with preventive COVID-19 measures," PsyPost website, April 2, 2022, https://www.psypost.org/2022/04/large-study-finds-closed-mindedness-predicts-non-compliance-with-preventive-covid-19-measures-62833/

28 Jarrett, How to foster

29 Elizabeth J. Krumrei-Mancuso, Megan C. Haggard, Jordan P. LaBouff & Wade C. Rowatt (2020) Links between intellectual humility and acquiring knowledge, The Journal of Positive Psychology, 15:2, 155-170, DOI: 10.1080/17439760.2019.1579359 https://tandfonline.com/doi/full/10.1080/17439760.2019.1579359/

30 Krumrei-Mancuso, E. J., & Rouse, S. V. (2016). The Development and Validation of the Comprehensive Intellectual Humility Scale. Journal of Personality Assessment, 98, 209–221. https://doi.org/10.1080/00223891.2015.1068174

Chapter 5: The Growth Mindmap: It's All in Your Mind… Set

1   Carol Dweck, *Mindset: The New Psychology of Success*. Updated Edition (New York: Ballantine Books), 2007.

2   "Dr. Dweck's research into growth mindset changed education forever," Mindset Works website, https://www.mindsetworks.com/science/

3   Dweck, Mindset

4   Kendra Cherry, "What Is a Mindset and Why It Matters," VeryWellMind website, updated on September 20, 2022, https://www.verywellmind.com/what-is-a-mindset-2795025/

5   Craig Impelman, "You Are Not a Failure Until You Start Blaming Others for Your Mistakes," TheWoodenEffect.com, May 20, 2018, https://www.thewoodeneffect.com/blaming-others/

6   Dweck, Mindset, p 33.

7   Elizabeth Pratt, "6 Ways to Rewire Your Brain," Healthline website, June 11, 2020, https://www.healthline.com/health/growth-mindset-neuroplasticity

8   Lynne Levy, "How to Use the Growth Mindset Feedback Approach to Improve Performance," Workhuman website, October 17, 2022, https://www.workhuman.com/blog/growth-mindset-feedback/

9   Anne-Laure Le Cunff, "From fixed mindset to growth mindset: the complete guide," Ness Labs website, https://nesslabs.com/growth-mindset/

10 Zainab, "5 Ways To Deal With Uncertainty,"Medium, February 18, 2018, https://zainabwrites.medium.com/5-fives-to-deal-with-uncertainty-69f77eaabb2d/

11 Roy T. Bennett, *The Light in the Heart*, Roy T. Bennett publisher, November, 2021.

12 Dweck, Mindset, p 11.

13 Carol Dweck, "The power of yet," TEDxNorrköping, September 12, 2014, accessed at: https://www.youtube.com/watch?v=J-swZaKN2lc/

Chapter 6: The Wonder of Awe

1   H B Gelatt, "The Power of Wonder," December 10, 2019, https://hbgelatt.wordpress.com/2019/12/10/the-power-of-wonder/

2   Mei, Yi Pao, "Mencius," The New Encyclopedia Britannica, v. 8, 1985,.p. 3.

3   "The Most Common Questions that Kids Ask," You Are Mom website, https://youaremom.com/parenting/common-questions-that-kids-ask/

4   Rachel Carson, The Sense of Wonder (New York: Harper Collins), 1998.

5   Walter Isaacson, Einstein: His Life and Universe, (New York: Simon & Schuster), 2007.

6   Jonathon McPhetres (2019). Oh, the things you don't know: awe promotes awareness of knowledge gaps and science interest, Cognition and Emotion, 33:8, 1599-1615, DOI: 10.1080/02699931.2019.1585331, https://www.tandfonline.com/doi/full/10.1080/02699931.2019.1585331/; also Daniel Stancato and Dacher Keltner, "Awe, ideological conviction, and perceptions of ideological opponents," APA PsycNet, Emotion, Vol 21(1), Feb 2021, 61-72, https://psycnet.apa.org/buy/2019-46364-001/

7   Mary Davis page, Goodreads, https://www.goodreads.com/author/show/19977202.Mary_Davis/

8   Stephen DeAngelis, "Wonder and Curiosity Make the World Go Around," Enterra Solutions website, April 15, 2022, https://enterrasolutions.com/wonder-and-curiosity-make-the-world-go-around/

9   Albert Einstein, "Old Man's Advice to Youth: 'Never Lose a Holy Curiosity'," Life, May 2, 1955, p 64.

10 Samantha Green, "Why Curiosity and Wonder Are Critical for the Next Generation of Scientists," Wiley website, https://www.wiley.com/en-us/network/publishing/societies/research-impact/why-curiosity-and-wonder-are-critical-for-the-next-generation-of-scientists

11 Kelli Boyle, "'Ted Lasso' Dart Scene Was Perfected Last-Minute by Jason Sudeikis, Hannah Waddingham Says," ShowBiz Cheat Sheet website, July 26, 2021, https://www.cheatsheet.com/entertainment/ted-lasso-dart-scene-perfected-last-minute-jason-sudeikis-hannah-waddingham-says.html/

12 Li J-J, Dou K, Wang Y-J and Nie Y-G (2019) Why Awe Promotes Prosocial Behaviors? The Mediating Effects of Future Time Perspective and Self-Transcendence Meaning of Life. *Front. Psychol.* 10:1140. doi: 10.3389/fpsyg.2019.01140; Rudd M, Vohs KD, Aaker J. Awe expands people's perception of time, alters decision making, and enhances well-being. Psychol Sci. 2012 Oct 1;23(10):1130-6. doi: 10.1177/0956797612438731. Epub 2012 Aug 10. PMID: 22886132; Paul K. Piff, et al, "Awe, the Small Self, and Prosocial Behavior," Journal of Personality and Social Psychology © 2015 American Psychological Association 2015, Vol. 108, No. 6, 883–899; Bai Y, Maruskin LA, Chen S, Gordon AM, Stellar JE, McNeil GD, Peng K, Keltner D. Awe, the diminished self, and collective engagement: Universals and cultural variations in the small self. J Pers Soc Psychol. 2017 Aug;113(2):185-209. doi: 10.1037/pspa0000087. Epub 2017 May 8. PMID: 28481617.

13 Raymond J. Corsini, *Encyclopedia of Psychology* (Hoboken: John Wiley & Sons), 1998.

14 Rathee Singh, Neelam & Dhillon, Sukhmani. (2021). Self-transcendence, Mindfulness and Virtues. 13. 53–65.

15 Darcia F. Narvaez, "Self-Actualization: Are You on the Path?," Psychology Today, February 11, 2018. https://www.psychologytoday.com/us/blog/moral-landscapes/201802/self-actualization-are-you-the-path/

16 Ruth Hartt "Transcendence and awe: It's not for everyone," Ruth Hartt website, https://www.cultureforhire.com/articles/transcendence-and-awe/

17 Ibid.

18 A. H. Maslow, "A Theory of Human Motivation," Psychological Review, 50, 370–396, 1943. Accessed online at: http://psychclassics.yorku.ca/Maslow/motivation.htm

19 Mary West, "Maslow's hierarchy of needs: Uses and criticisms," MedicalNewsToday website, July 29, 2022, https://www.medicalnewstoday.com/articles/maslows-hierarchy-of-needs/

20 Scott Barry Kaufman "Who Created Maslow's Iconic Pyramid?," Scientific American, April 23, 2019, https://blogs.scientificamerican.com/beautiful-minds/who-created-maslows-iconic-pyramid/

21 Matt Davis, "Maslow's Forgotten Pinacle: Self-Transcendence," Big Think, August 9, 2019, https://bigthink.com/neuropsych/maslow-self-transcendence/

22 Abraham H. Maslow, The Farther Reaches of Human Nature (New York: The Viking Press). 1971, p. 269.

23 Courtney E. Ackerman, "What Is Self-Transcendence?" PositivePsychology.com, June 4, 2018,
https://positivepsychology.com/self-transcendence/

Chapter 7: Receive

1 "Brain works like a radio receiver," *Science Daily*, January 22, 2014,
https://www.sciencedaily.com/releases/2014/01/140122133713.htm

2 "ELEMENTS AND CHARACTERISTICS OF TREND," SlideShare, November 10, 2017,
https://www.slideshare.net/CenthiameBelonio/elements-and-characteristics-of-trend/

3 https://emtemp.gcom.cloud/ngw/globalassets/en/articles/images/hype-cycle-for-emerging-tech-2022.png

4 Andy McGregor Vision and strategy toolkit, Jisc website, November 3, 2020,
https://www.jisc.ac.uk/guides/vision-and-strategy-toolkit/trends-analysis/

5 How to Identify Market Trends for Long-Term Business Planning, Course Hero, February 7, 2022,
https://www.coursehero.com/file/129058906/How-to-identify-market-trends-for-longdocx/

6 Heer Patel, "The Difference between Micro- and Macro-trends," accessed on LinkedIn, posted January 23, 2022, https://www.linkedin.com/pulse/fashion-moves-fast-how-can-we-keep-up-heer-patel/; see also
https://blog.shrm.org/blog/future-friday-can-you-tell-the-difference-between-fads-micro-trends-macro-t/

7 Kathy Borlik, "Pickleball leads to love-love game, set, marriage," South Bend Tribune, September 19, 2022,
https://www.southbendtribune.com/story/news/2022/09/19/pickleball-leads-to-love-love-and-marriage-for-osceola-couple/69487042007/

8 Bryce Airgood, "As pickleball's popularity grows, tennis players left to fight for their courts," *Lansing State Journal*, February 8, 2023,
https://www.lansingstatejournal.com/story/news/local/2023/02/09/pickleball-tennis-players-fight-over-courts/69845803007/

9 Thomas J. Ryan, "EXEC: Is Pickleball Losing Its Pandemic Bump?," SGB Media website, March 31, 2023,
https://sgbonline.com/exec-is-pickleball-losing-its-pandemic-bump/

10 "APP Reveals 36.5 Million Adult Americans Played Pickleball In 2022," APP website, January 4, 2023,
https://www.theapp.global/news/app-reveals-36-5-million-adult-americans-played-pickleball-in-2022#:~:text=The%20headline%20numbers%20include%2014,times%20or%20more%20in%202022.

11 Airgood, As Picketball's

12 Patel, The Difference Between

13 Joel Alcedo, et al, "Pandemic's E-commerce Surge Proves Less Persistent, More Varied," IMF Blog, March 17, 2022,
https://www.imf.org/en/Blogs/Articles/2022/03/17/pandemics-e-commerce-surge-proves-less-persistent-more-varied/

14 Patel, The Difference Between

15 Jan Burch, "What Is a Macro Trend?," It Still Works website, updated August 23, 2018, https://yourbusiness.azcentral.com/macro-trend-8289.html

16 April Montgomery and Ken Mingis, "The evolution of Apple's iPhone," *ComputerWorld*, November 13, 2023, https://www.computerworld.com/article/3692531/evolution-of-apple-iphone.html

17 Chris Smith. "What were the most popular phones of 2006, and how do they stack up today?" Decluttr Blog, November 21, 2016, https://www.decluttr.com/blog/2016/11/21/what-were-the-most-popular-phones-of-2006-and-how-do-they-stack-up-today/

18 Arol Wright, "The first Android phone was announced 13 years ago today," Android Police website, September 23, 2021 https://www.androidpolice.com/2021/09/23/the-first-android-phone-was-announced-13-years-ago-today/

19 Chenda Ngak, "Then and Now: A History of Social Networking Sites," CBS News website, July 6, 2011, https://www.cbsnews.com/pictures/then-and-now-a-history-of-social-networking-sites/

20 Niraj Chokshi, "Myspace, Once the King of Social Networks, Lost Years of Data From Its Heyday," *New York Times*, March 19, 2019, accessed online: https://www.nytimes.com/2019/03/19/business/myspace-user-data.html

21 Mythili Devarakonda, "'The Social Network': When was Facebook created? How long did it take to create Facebook?," USA Today, July 25, 2022, accessed online: https://www.usatoday.com/story/tech/2022/07/25/when-was-facebook-created/10040883002/

22 Kate Johanns, "Tech Time Warp: Twitter Takes Flight at SXSW 2007," SmarterMsp, March 13, 2020, https://smartermsp.com/tech-time-warp-twitter-takes-flight-at-sxsw-2007/

23 Dan Blystone, "Instagram: What It Is, Its History, and How the Popular App Works," Investopedia, January 12, 2014, https://www.investopedia.com/articles/investing/102615/story-instagram-rise-1-photo0sharing-app.asp

24 Brian O'Connell, "History of Snapchat: Timeline and Facts," The Street, February 8, 2020, https://www.thestreet.com/technology/history-of-snapchat/

25 "7 macro trends shaping the future of work," DeskBird website, September 15, 2021 Updated: April 13, 2023 deskbird.com/blog/7-macro-trends-shaping-the-future-of-work/

26 "The Megatrends," ZukunftsInstitute website, December 19, 2023, https://www.zukunftsinstitut.de/zukunftsthemen/dossier/megatrends-en

27 Paul Kirvan and Ivy Wigmore, "What is a microtrend?" TechTarget website, https://www.techtarget.com/whatis/definition/microtrend

28 "Futures Thinking & Foresight," Turian Labs website, https://www.turianlabs.com/megatrends-1

29 "What are megatrends?" BlackRock website, https://blackrock.com/sg/en/investment-ideas/themes/megatrends/

30 Kate Baggaley, "Self-Driving Cars Will Create Organ Shortage – Can Science Meet Demand?" NBC News website, February 10, 2017, https://www.nbcnews.com/mach/science/can-science-curb-donor-organ-shortage-self-driving-cars-will-n719386/

31 April Dembosky, "Organ Transplants Down As Stay-At-Home Rules Reduce Fatal Traffic Collisions," NPR News, May 20, 2020, https://www.npr.org/sections/health-shots/2020/05/20/858712314/organ-transplants-down-as-stay-at-home-rules-reduce-fatal-traffic-collisions/

32 Trevor English, "Why Driverless Cars Might Cause an Organ Shortage," Interesting Engineering website, February 4, 2020, https://interestingengineering.com/innovation/why-driverless-cars-might-cause-an-organ-shortage/

33 Sue Whitbread, "What is ChatGPT and why is AI suddenly a big deal? Analysis from WisdomTree's Global Head of Research," IFA Magazine website, March 14, 2023, https://ifamagazine.com/article/what-is-chatgpt-and-why-is-ai-suddenly-a-big-deal-analysis-from-wisdomtrees-global-head-of-research/

34 What are megatrends? BlackRock

35 Lori Perri, "What's New in the 2022 Gartner Hype Cycle for Emerging Technologies," Gartner website, August 10, 2022 https://www.gartner.com/en/articles/what-s-new-in-the-2022-gartner-hype-cycle-for-emerging-technologies/

36 "Gartner Hype Cycle," Gartner website, gartner.com/en/research/methodologies/gartner-hype-cycle/

37 "Design Thinking Defined," DesignThinkingIdeo.com, https://designthinking.ideo.com/

38 "What's the difference between human-centered design and design thinking?" in Frequently Asked Questions, on DesignThinkingIdeo.com, https://designthinking.ideo.com/faq/whats-the-difference-between-human-centered-design-and-design-thinking/

Chapter 8: Perceive

1   "H1 vs H2 vs H3: What's the Difference Between Them? Learn it Here," June 22, 2021, RockContent blog, https://rockcontent.com/blog/h1-vs-h2/

Chapter 9: Weave

1   Scott Galloway, "Storytelling," ProfGalloway.com website, May 5, 2023, https://www.profgalloway.com/storytelling/

2   "Michael Lewis's 9 Rules of Storytelling," Next Big Idea Club, December 23, 2016, https://nextbigideaclub.com/magazine/michael-lewiss-9-rules-storytelling/20462/

3   Ron Ploof, "A Story Is" video, accessed at: https://www.youtube.com/watch?v=dti2nmUybo8

4   Daniel Van Boom, "iPhone 12 launch day: People are still lining up for Apple's new devices," CNET, October 23, 2020, https://www.cnet.com/tech/mobile/iphone-12-launch-day-people-are-still-lining-up-for-apples-new-devices/

5   Merriam Webster Dictionary, https://www.merriam-webster.com/dictionary/narrative

6   "Gain Focus, Gain Traction," Metahelm website, https://www.metahelm.com/about

7   Guillaume Wiatr, "Story vs. Narrative? And Why It Matters," Metahelm website, September 2, 2020, metahelm.com/blog/84563-story-vs-narrative-and-why-it-matters

8   Cambridge Dictionary, https://dictionary.cambridge.org/us/dictionary/english/weave

9   Sandy McDonald website, https://sandymcdonald.com/contextualized-storytelling-builds-trust

10 "Oxytocin: The Love Hormone," Harvard Health Publishing website, June 13, 2023, https://www.health.harvard.edu/mind-and-mood/oxytocin-the-love-hormone

11 "Oxytocin," Cleveland Clinic website, https://my.clevelandclinic.org/health/articles/22618-oxytocin

12 "IKEA apps," Ikea website, https://www.ikea.com/au/en/customer-service/mobile-apps/say-hej-to-ikea-place-pub1f8af050

13 Replacement citation to come. https://www.effectivetrainingsolutions.com/etsblog/what-is-essential-is-invisible-to-the-eyes

14 Brian Solis Twitter post, May 31, 2023, https://twitter.com/briansolis/status/1663925079967936512

15 "Steps 2 & 3: Critical uncertainties," FutureLearn website, https://www.futurelearn.com/info/courses/presenting-your-work-with-impact/0/steps/

16 "Brian Gregg Peter, "6 Rules of Great Storytelling (As Told by Pixar)," https://briangreggpeters.com/storytelling

17 "What Are Spider Graphs?" The Plaid Horse website, https://www.theplaidhorse.com/2022/10/05/what-are-spider-graphs/

18 "Preparing for the Future: The Power of Scenario Planning," Jedox website, https://www.jedox.com/wp-content/pdf/jedox-ebook-scenario-planning-en.pdf

19 Peter Schwartz, "The Futurist Equation: 2122," BigThink website, https://bigthink.com/progress/plan-for-progress-peter-schwartz/

20 Ibid.

21 Surabhi Rawat, "7 Interesting Facts About the Hitchhikers' Guide to the Galaxy," Times of India, March 11, 2023, https://timesofindia.indiatimes.com/life-style/books/web-stories/7-interesting-facts-about-douglas-adams-and-the-hitchhikers-guide-to-the-galaxy/photostory/98568871

22 Paul Bignell, "42: The answer to life, the universe and everything," Independent, February 6, 2011, https://www.independent.co.uk/life-style/history/42-the-answer-to-life-the-universe-and-everything-2205734.html

23 "The Hitchhiker's Guide to the Galaxy," BBC Radio 4, https://www.bbc.co.uk/programmes/profiles/wqGHb88RDCJ2j8hXGwgBYn/deep-thought

24 Peter Loshin, "ASCII (American Standard Code for Information Interchange)," TechTarget Network website, https://www.techtarget.com/whatis/definition/ASCII-American-Standard-Code-for-Information-Interchange

25 "The meaning of Life, the Universe and Everything," posted by Badwolf582 on Reddit, https://www.reddit.com/r/FanTheories/comments/19botr/the_meaning_of_life_the_universe_and_everything/

26 "The truth behind 42 being the meaning of life, the universe and everything. 95% sure this is true," posted on Reddit, https://www.reddit.com/r/FanTheories/comments/24uio5/the_truth_behind_42_being_the_meaning_of_life_the/?rdt=43920

Chapter 10: Conceive

1   Hang Xu, posted on LinkedIn, https://www.linkedin.com/feed/update/urn:li:activity:7067498265667072002/

2   Margaret Banford,"Cassandra Complex in Mythology, Psychology, and the Modern World," Learning Mind website, December 27, 2018, https://www.learning-mind.com/cassandra-complex/

3   Ibid.

4   Theron Mohamed, "'Big Short' investor Michael Burry says Warren Buffett is unique — and being different is key to investing success," Yahoo Finance, May 23, 2022, success," https://finance.yahoo.com/news/big-short-investor-michael-burry-150852638.html

5   Shawn Callahan, "What Makes a Compelling Story? Here are 6 Key Elements," Anecdote website, September 19, 2018, https://www.anecdote.com/2018/09/what-makes-a-compelling-story/

6   Brian G. Peters, "6 Rules of Great Storytelling (As Told by Pixar)," Medium, March 21, 2018, https://medium.com/@Brian_G_Peters/6-rules-of-great-storytelling-as-told-by-pixar-fcc6ae225f50

7   "The 22 Pixar Storytelling Rules: Lessons for Screenwriters," Industrial Scripts website, August 2, 2022, https://industrialscripts.com/pixar-storytelling-rules/

8   Design 2 Blog, Parsons School of Design, "Story Boards," https://parsonsdesign2.wordpress.com/resources/story-boards/

9   Bronwyn Fryer, "Storytelling That Moves People," Harvard Business Review, June 2003, https://hbr.org/2003/06/storytelling-that-moves-people

10 Robert McKee, Story: Substance, Structure, Style and the Principles of Screenwriting (New York: Harper Collins), 1997. p. 12.

11 Peters, 6 Rules

12 Chris Hewitt, "Minnesota native Pete Docter turned his life into Pixar movies 'Toy Story,' 'Up' and 'Soul'," StarTribune, November 23, 2020, https://www.startribune.com/minnesota-native-pete-docter-turned-his-life-into-pixar-movies-toy-story-up-and-soul/573166761

13 "David Majister, "Tell Stories like Pixar's Greatest Movie Director," Medium, May 5, 2021, https://medium.com/publishous/tell-stories-like-pixars-greatest-movie-director-a49448dc582c

14 Ibid.

15 Fryer, Storytelling that Moves

16 Ibid.

17 https://chat.openai.com/
    Prompt: You are a professor in business school. you are preparing a special lesson that helps emerging leaders in business convince executives that trends are on the horizon that may bring disruption to their company. you want to help them creatively solve their problem. your idea is to help them become Pixar storytellers. what are the 7 plot types that your students, emerging leaders, can use to make the case for change.

18 Khan Academy, Pixar in a Box course, Lesson 1: We are all storytellers, https://www.khanacademy.org/computing/pixar/storytelling/we-are-all-storytellers/v/video3-final

19 For Folks Who Can't Plot: Use "Story Spine" 7-step method, posted by kschang on Reddit, https://www.reddit.com/r/writing/comments/13l3geo/for_folks_who_cant_plot_use_story_spine_7step/

20 Yves Lummer, "Story Spine: A Powerful 8-Step Storytelling Structure," Book Bird website, March 26, 2023, https://bookbird.io/story-spine/

21 "The Story Spine from Kenn Adams," video accessed: https://www.youtube.com/watch?v=pRHXVbsuAQw

22 Kenn Adams, "Back to the Story Spine," Aerogramme Writers Studio website, June 5, 2013, https://www.aerogrammestudio.com/2013/06/05/back-to-the-story-spine/

23 Joseph Campbell, The Hero With a Thousand Faces (New York: New World Library), 2008.

24 Lisa Fritscher "Carl Jung's Collective Unconscious Theory: What It Suggests About the Mind," VeryWellMind website, May 17, 2023, verywellmind.com/what-is-the-collective-unconscious-2671571

25 Dan Bronzite "The Hero's Journey - Mythic Structure of Joseph Campbell's Monomyth," Movie Outline website, https://www.movieoutline.com/articles/the-hero-journey-mythic-structure-of-joseph-campbell-monomyth.html

26 All quotes of Vogler from Christopher Vogler, "The Memo That Started It All," https://livingspirit.typepad.com/files/chris-vogler-memo-1.pdf

27 Hero's journey description derived from "The Writer's Journey: Mythic Structure for Writers," Course Hero, January 22, 2020, coursehero.com/file/53660362/The-Writers-Journey-Mythic-Structure-for-Writerspdf/

28 Bronzite, The Hero's Journey

29 Brad Montague, "Keynote, Fall CUE 2017," Bigspeak Speakers Bureau, https://www.youtube.com/watch?v=uPfq_zGBwOI
Brad Montague Twitter post, January 11, 2021, https://twitter.com/thebradmontague/status/1348793930582777859

Chapter 11: Believe

1 Sarah Kessler "How Snow White Helped AirBnb's Mobile Mission," Fast Company, November 8, 2012, https://www.fastcompany.com/1681924/how-snow-white-helped-airbnbs-mobile-mission

2 Nathan Blecharczyk, "Visualizing the Customer Experience," Sequoia website, https://articles.sequoiacap.com/visualizing-customer-experience

3 Simon Sinek, "If The CEO Speaks, Make Sure He Says Why," HuffPost, May 16, 2010, https://www.huffpost.com/entry/if-the-ceo-speaks-make-su_b_501490

4 Zach Gemignani, "The Art of Data Storytelling," JuiceAnalytics website, May 1, 2021, https://www.juiceanalytics.com/writing/the-art-of-data-storytelling-pixar-style

5   Parsons, Design2, Storyboards,
    https://parsonsdesign2.wordpress.com/resources/story-boards/

6   Holly Riddle, "The 8 Point Story Arc: What It Is and How to Use This Story Structure,"
    Scribophile website,
    https://www.scribophile.com/academy/what-is-the-8-point-story-arc

7   "Instances of the "You're probably wondering how I got here" movie trope being used in
    movies - Was it ever a trope?," posted on Reddit by GalacticAccident,
    https://www.reddit.com/r/MandelaEffect/comments/khsg39/instances_of_the_
    youre_probably_wondering_how_i/

8   Venecia Williams, "Chapter 4: Organizing Your Ideas," Fundamentals of Business
    Communication, BCCampus website, https://pressbooks.bccampus.ca/
    businesswritingessentials/chapter/ch-5-organizing-your-ideas/

9   "Writing Effective Impact Statements," Virginia Tech website, https://www
    .communications.cals.vt.edu/resources/impact-statements.html

10 Dolan, The Hero's Journey

Chapter 12: Achieve

1   Make Something Wonderful: Steve Jobs in His Own Words, https://book
    .stevejobsarchive.com/

2   Goodreads quotes page, Vince Lombardi, goodreads.com/quotes/11114711-to-me-a-
    leader-is-a-visionary-that-energizes-others

3   "Culture's Role In Enabling Organizational Change," PriceWatersHouseCooper website,
    https://www.strategyand.pwc.com/gx/en/insights/2011-2014/cultures-role-
    organizational-change.html

4   Brian Westfall "Change is Making Employee Burnout Worse," Capterra website, June 6,
    2022, https://www.capterra.com/resources/change-fatigue-in-the-workplace/

5   Everett Rogers, The Diffusion of Innovations, 5th Edition (New York: Free Press), 2003.

6   Greg Satell, "To Implement Change, You Don't Need to Convince Everyone at Once,"
    Harvard Business Review, May 11, 2023,
    https://hbr.org/2023/05/to-implement-change-you-dont-need-to-convince-everyone-
    at-once

7   Goodreads, Peter Senge quotes,
    https://www.goodreads.com/quotes/125720-people-don-t-resist-change-they-resist-
    being-changed

8   Dale Carnegie, How to Win Friends and Influence People (New York: Simon & Schuster),
    2022.

9   "The Best Summary of How to Win Friends and Influence People," FS Blog,
    https://fs.blog/how-to-win-friends-and-influence-people/

10 "What does the gesture in art of the finger pointing upwards mean?," StackExchange
    website,
    https://crafts.stackexchange.com/questions/10354/what-does-the-gesture-in-art-of-
    the-finger-pointing-upwards-mean

11 Keith Ferrazzi, Embrace Relationship Action Planning (RAP),"posted on LinkedIn, June 12, 2014,
    https://www.linkedin.com/pulse/20140612171618-1052611-want-better-meetings-
    embrace-relationship-action-planning-rap/

12 Ibid.

13 Ibid.

14 Rasmus Hougaard and Jacqueline Carter, "Ego Is the Enemy of Good Leadership," Harvard Business Review, November 6, 2018, https://hbr.org/2018/11/ego-is-the-enemy-of-good-leadership

15 Executive Blind Spots: Discrepancies Between Self- and Other-Ratings, October 2003, Consulting Psychology Journal, Practice and Research, 55(4):222–229 DOI:10.1037/1061-4087.55.4.222

16 Golden, James L.; Berquist, Goodwin F.; Coleman, William E.; Sproule, J. Michael, eds. (2010) [1976]. The rhetoric of Western thought: From the Mediterranean world to the global setting (10th ed.). Dubuque, Iowa: Kendall Hunt. p. 67.

17 The Visual Communication Guy website, https://thevisualcommunicationguy.com/rhetoric-overview/the-rhetorical-appeals-rhetorical-triangle/

18 "Pathos, Logos, and Ethos," St. Louis Community College website, https://stlcc.edu/student-support/academic-success-and-tutoring/writing-center/writing-resources/pathos-logos-and-ethos.aspx

19 Jennifer Aker and Naomi Bagdonas, *Humor, Seriously* (New York: Crown Curreny) 2021. Book website: https://www.humorseriously.com/

20 Jennifer Aaker and Naomi Bagdonas, "Why great Leaders Take Humor Seriously" TedX Warrenton, https://www.tedxwarrenton.com/2022/01/17/why-great-leaders-take-humor-seriously-by-jennifer-aaker-and-naomi-bagdonas/

21 Cindy Weiner, Humor,Seriously, Maria Shriver website, ://mariash shriver.com/humor-seriously/

22 The Visual Communication Guy, https://thevisualcommunicationguy.com/rhetoric-overview/the-rhetorical-appeals-rhetorical-triangle/

23 Ian Birrell, review of *You Talkin' to Me? Rhetoric From Aristotle to Obama*, October 15, 2011, https://www.theguardian.com/books/2011/oct/16/talking-me-aristotle-obama-review

24 Ibid.

25 John Nichols, "Obama's 3 Million Vote," The Nation, November 9, 2012, https://www.thenation.com/article/archive/obamas-3-million-vote-electoral-college-landslide-majority-states-mandate/

26 Ibid.

27 Mylena Vocal Coach, "Why Mylena Vocal Coach, President Barack Obama is One of the Greatest Speakers in the World?," InbornVoice website, https://www.inbornvoice.com/us/News/why-president-barack-obama-is-one-of-the-greatest-speakers-in-the-world

28 Richard Feloni, "2015 World Championship of Public Speaking," *Business Insider*, Septembr 11, 2015, https://www.businessinsider.com/toastmasters-public-speaking-champion-mohammed-qahtani-2015-9

29 Michael Potuck "Jony Ive discusses the importance and absurdity between leveraging 'curiosity' and the focus to 'solve problems'," 9to5Mac website, November 20, 2018, https://9to5mac.com/2018/11/20/jony-ive-discusses-the-importance-and-absurdity-between-leveraging-curiosity-and-the-focus-to-solve-problems/

30 Zameena Mejia, "Steve Jobs almost prevented the Apple iPhone from being invented," CNBC Make It website, September 12, 2017, https://www.cnbc.com/2017/09/12/why-steve-jobs-almost-prevented-the-apple-iphone-from-being-invented.html

31 Alan Trapulionis, "Steve Jobs Initially Hated the iPhone Idea," Medium, March 14, 2022, https://alan-12169.medium.com/how-steve-jobs-almost-killed-the-iphone-5f9bccb27bab

32 Benj Edwards, "The iPod: How Apple's legendary portable music player came to be," Macworld, October 22, 2011 https://ww.macworld. com/article/189142/ipodsales-3.html

33 Dean Takahashi, "Nest CEO Tony Fadell on the iPod, iPhone and the Importance of Shipping Products," VentureBeat, February 28, 2016, https://venturebeat.com/business/how-the-father-of-the-ipod-iphone-and-nest-became-a-tech-visionary/

34 Silvio Deda, "Steve Jobs almost prevented the iPhone from being created," Silvio Deda website, March 9, 2023, https://www.silviodeda.com/steve-jobs-almost-prevented-the-iphone-from-being-created/

35 Brian Merchant, *The One Device*, (New York: Little Brown and Company), 2017, p 202.

36 Merchant, One Device, p 205.

37 Jack Morse, "The iPhone Almost Looked Completely Different," Mashable, June 14, 2017, https://mashable.com/article/iphone-apple-steve-jobs-ipod

38 Stan Schroeder, "How an iPod with a Rotary Eventually Became the iPhone," Mashable, March 1, 2016, https://mashable.com/article/ipod-iphone-rotary-dial-tony-fadell

Conclusion: If Not You, Who?

1 https://essence.com/news/denzel-washington-commencement-honorary-doctorate-upenn-university-of-pennsylvania/

2 https://youtube.com/watch?v=QyDo5vFD2R8

3 "Megginson in the Field," Natinal Center for Science Education website, August 26, 2015, https://ncse.ngo/megginson-field

4 "13 inspiring Roald Dahl quotes," Penguin Books website, https://www.penguin.co.uk/articles/childrens-article/inspiring-roald-dahl-quotes

Credits

Credits

p 8   Inspired by Gapingvoid Culture Design Group.

P 30   1968 Ford GT40 Mk I. Courtesy Creative Commons. Photo by Sicnag. Ford GPT Leading the Race at Le Mans. Courtesy Creative Commons. Photo provided by HYPERLINK "https://www.flickr.com/people/44865643@N07"ZANTAFIO56.

P 33   Both images courtesy Adobe Stock.

P 34   Image from Carscoops website, image at left from XenTR, at right from T-Tech Solutions LLC.

P 106 Adobe Stock, image by sadia.

P 124 Inspired by GapingVoid.

P 138 Adobe Stock.

P 189 Redrawn from image posted by Hang Xu at: https://www.linkedin.com/feed/update/urn:li:activity:7067498265667072002/

P 220 Images courtesy of Nick Sung.

P 224 Images courtesy of Nick Sung.

P 254 Wikimedia Commons, courtesy of Wogone.

P 256 Image from Apple patent filings, reproduced in the post "Steve Jobs Secret Meeting to Explore an iPod Phone is Revealing," on the PatentlyApple website: https://www.patentlyapple.com/2011/11/steve-jobs-secret-meeting-to-explore-an-ipod-phone-is-revealing.html

286

Index

N

Nan-in (Zen master), 76
Narrative, 192
  arch, 232–233
  definition, 167
  weaving, 168
Naysayers, mindshifter battles, 23
Negativity
  combatting, 58–64
  consumption, brain wiring, 59
  contagion, 61
  resistance category, 239
  self-reflection, 60
  transformation, 61–63
Networking, importance, 244
Ni, Daoshing, 75
Nietzsche, Friedrich, 36
Nike, storyboarding (usage), 222–223
Nin, Anaïs, 5
Novel Economy, 6
  propulsion, 22

O

Obama, Barack
  rhetorical power, 251
  speeches, 250–251
Omnichannel retail, research, 216–218
One Device: The Secret History of the iPhone
  (Merchant), 254
Open mind, 242
  benefit, 77–78
Opportunities
  approach/discovery, 72, 125
  cost, score, 177
  observations, 261
  vicious cycle, 92–93
  virtuous cycle, 95
  wealth, capitalization, 5
Optimism
  development, 58, 60
  increase, 58
  self-reflection, 60
Optimism, cultivation, 58–64
Ordeal/supreme ordeal (hero journey
  element), 207–208
Ordinary world
  departure (hero journey element),
    205–206
  return (hero journey element), 209–210

Origgi, Mylena, 251
O'Toole, James, 56
Outcomes
  desire, 7
  improvement, belief, 43
  reimagining, 5
  results, 77
Outlook
  decision, 58
  restriction, 60
Overconfidence bias, 65
Owyang, Jeremiah, 172

P

Page, Larry, 26
Parking lot
  creation, 144
  usage, 145, 148, 152, 153
Participation, importance, 130
Passion, importance, 46
Pathos (Aristotle), 247–250, 253
Patterns
  categorization, 150–153
  discovery, 146
  technology themes, 148
Peak experiences, 113
Perceive (mindset shifting stage), 123, 144
Persistence, courage, 100
Perspective
  vicious cycle, 92
  virtuous cycle, 94
Pixar, 170–171, 200–201, 215
  mindshifting approach, 219–221
  storyboard work, 225
Pleasers (leadership archetype), 57
Ploof, Ron, 167
Plot, problems, 197–199
Positive people/inputs, impact, 63
Potential ROI, score, 178–179
PowerPoint, usage, 225
Predictive consumerism, 161, 162
Pressfield, Steven, 47–48
Prime Music, 50
Prime Video, 50
Prioritization (trends), 145, 157–163
Problems
  approach, 72
  default reactions, 58
Problem-solvers, traits (differences), 41
Productivity, plateau, 139